FIX IT and FLIP IT

How to Make Money Rehabbing REAL ESTATE for PROFIT

KATIE HAMILTON AND GENE HAMILTON

McGraw·Hill

New York   Chicago   San Francisco   Lisbon   London   Madrid   Mexico City
Milan   New Delhi   San Juan   Seoul   Singapore   Sydney   Toronto

Library of Congress Cataloging-in-Publication Data

Hamilton, Katie.
    Fix it and flip it : how to make money rehabbing real estate for profit / Katie Hamilton
and Gene Hamilton.
        p.   cm.
    Includes index.
    ISBN 0-07-142148-3 (pbk. : alk. paper)
    1. Real estate investment—United States.   2. House buying—United States.
3. House selling—United States.   4. Dwellings—Remodeling—United States.
5. Housing rehabilitation—Economic aspects—United States.   I. Hamilton, Gene.
II. Title.

HD255.H294   2004
332.63'24'0973—dc22   2004000952

We dedicate this book to the memory of Jane Jordan Browne, our friend and agent. Twenty years ago when we met Jane and wanted to take the leap from magazine writing to books, she welcomed us into the world of book publishing. Our personal and business relationship with Jane grew and flourished as her quick wit and sage advice guided and counseled us along the way. We are fortunate to have known her all these years.

8 9 10 11 12 13   FGR/FGR   3 2 1 0 9 8 7 6

ISBN 0-07-142148-3

McGraw-Hill books are available at special quantity discounts to use as premiums and sales promotions, or for use in corporate training programs. For more information, please write to the Director of Special Sales, Professional Publishing, McGraw-Hill, Two Penn Plaza, New York, NY 10121-2298. Or contact your local bookstore.

This book is printed on acid-free paper.

CONTENTS

iii

CHAPTER 12 ESTIMATING FIX-UP COSTS

INTRODUCTION

In 1966 we bought our first fixer-upper—a two-bedroom brick duplex in much need of repair. We were schoolteachers by day and fledgling do-it-yourselfers by night, learning new skills (and making many mistakes) as we patched and painted and scraped and tiled. Year after year, house after house, our profits and confidence grew, and we turned to buying and working on houses full-time.

In the late 1970s we began writing magazine articles and books about home improvements. Our newspaper column, "Do It Yourself . . . Or Not?" (diyornot.com), has been syndicated by Tribune Media Services for the past 15 years. We took a leap into the online world in 1995 and created housenet.com, the first home-improvement channel on AOL.

Through the years we've continued to invest in real estate, and this book crystallizes what we've learned. Some investors define flipping as buying property and reselling it without taking possession. Our definition is buying a house that is distressed or undervalued, taking possession, making improvements to significantly raise its value, and then selling the house for a profit. In some cases after improving a house we find it has a greater value as a rental property, so we don't turn it over at all; we hold it for future earnings.

This book explains our investment strategy of finding a "good" house, or one that's ripe for rehabbing and flipping. We'll explain what we mean by "good" numbers, the formula we use to determine if there's a profit to be made.

You'll find worksheets that we've developed to evaluate a property and checklists to plan and manage a rehab project.

We've learned a lot about when to do a project yourself and when to hire contractors, and of course, we'll explain how investors can harness the power of the Internet to improve their investment decisions.

No one has published statistics of the number of rehabbing investors, but we know there are a lot of them. For years we've been meeting them at home shows where we've been speakers, on book tours across the country, and in online chat rooms on the Internet. They're young, urban Gen Xers, first-time suburban home owners, boomers, and empty nesters, all tackling fixer-uppers.

If you're ambitious and intrigued by the potential of rehabbing property, we hope you'll find the book useful and that it will lead you to a profitable venture investing in real estate.

CHAPTER 1

BUY, IMPROVE, AND SELL OR RENT TO PROFIT

How has your 401(k) or IRA performed in the past couple of years? Not so well, we suspect. Neither has ours, but the house we live in and another we rented and recently sold have done quite nicely. In fact, our $16,000 investment in the property we just sold earned us a $90,000 net profit. And during the time we owned the property we received a positive cash flow from rent.

There is a continual demand for housing, and the supply almost never keeps up with demand. When we first got married everyone we knew was either looking for an apartment to rent or a starter home to buy. We were both teaching school and had spare time on the weekends and summers to devote to improving what we bought, so investing in real estate also fit our lifestyle. Later on, when our jobs changed and we did not have as much time to devote to fixing up properties, we worked out a rent-and-hold strategy that fit our needs.

Creating Housing for the New Millennium

There were many opportunities to purchase properties when we started, and there still are today. The United States has 61 million houses that are at least 25 years old; 24 million are 16 to 25 years old. That's a lot of older houses with room for improvements. On top of that there's a home-improvement industry that is devoted to making the big job easier than ever. You've seen the growth of the do-it-yourself movement with the invasion of warehouse home centers and specialty home retailers wherever you live. Did you know the expenditures to improve, maintain, and repair the nation's 119 million homes totaled $214 billion in 2001? That's 2.1 percent of our nation's total economy.

We think what is driving this home-improvement boom is the desire to change older houses to fit a new lifestyle. Buyers today want kitchens and bathrooms that fit their more casual lifestyle. Just look at new houses that are built today. They have larger, family-oriented kitchens and more bathrooms that are more elaborate. Older houses that lack these desirable features are passed over by buyers.

Today's time-strapped home buyers are looking for a house they can move into and call their own without having to remodel and improve it. That point is illustrated by the long lines of buyers at open houses in popular neighborhoods and the speed with which many properties sell. But what about the houses that don't sell? Many are run down, and some come up short when compared to other properties in the market. But if you buy them right you can make money by improving them to meet buyers' expectations.

We've been doing that for many years—personally renovating 14 houses so far—and have never seen as many investment opportunities as there are today. You too can profit by investing in the right property and making improvements that yield a high appreciation and sell for a profit. This isn't rocket science; it's based on knowing how much to pay for a property, what kind of improvements to make, and how to sell or rent it at a profit. That's what this book is all about.

You're reading this chapter, so you are obviously intrigued by the possibility of profiting by rehabbing a house. This book will help you develop an investment strategy to find, buy, and improve property with payoff potential and explain how to maximize that potential.

You might be a fully employed individual who wants to build an investment strategy based on your place of residence. Over the years you can buy a house, live in and improve it, and then move up to a larger home—or just sell it and move someplace else. If you make the right improvements, you can pocket a hefty profit that is tax-free.

You might be a Gen Xer looking for a budget-priced house in an urban area or a suburban homeowner who sees the value of your home continue to rise so you want to invest in another one down the street. You might be a boomer looking in a beach town to rehab a second home to sell or rent, or maybe tackle a fixer-upper in the country, where you want to retire. Whatever your situation, investing in real estate can work for you.

What About You as an Investor?

The goal is to create a flexible investment strategy that works for you now and in the future as your life and career evolve. We've thought about this for a long time and are convinced it's all about your level of commitment, both *time* and *money*, and your *temperament*, *talents*, and *energy*. Let us explain.

Time

Do some soul-searching, or at least think about how much time you can reasonably devote to this venture. You might have to consult your significant other if you have one, or a potential partner. If you are time-challenged now, your best bet is to buy a house in a good location and live in it and work on it when you can. Inflation and the improvements you make will raise the value of the property.

If you do have some time to spare, you're in a good position to fix it and flip it. You can get in as deep as you want. Do the work yourself, supervise it, or hire it all out. You can make money in each situation.

Money

How much money do you have to invest? We have never used the no-money-down strategies, so you won't find that information here. Investing requires some capital, and we will suggest ways to raise the money and secure financing. And you won't hear us promising you can get rich quick in real estate, because we think it's hard work and takes time.

Personality

Now, about your temperament and talents. Let's be honest here. If you're high-strung and get stressed out when you're caught in traffic, you may have a difficult time rehabbing a house because there are many ups and downs you cannot control. If your talents naturally fall to managing people and details, you are most likely to succeed. If you like working with your hands and are gifted with tools, this is right up your alley. But if you're not handy, don't worry; there is more than enough work on the strategy end to keep you busy.

And how is your energy level connected to your real estate investment strategy? It's surprisingly simple. Rehabbing a house is a second job that takes considerable stamina, whether you're managing the work of others or doing it yourself. It's physical and emotional work that requires a high-energy person.

Investing in a House

We consider rehabbing a second job because it has all the components of a business. It is a business for many investors who have over the years parlayed their profits into buying and selling more properties. You'll have to decide at what level you're comfortable, but we'll give you a foundation to build on. We'll help you decide your strategy and level of commitment.

To begin with, we'll help you investigate neighborhoods and housing markets where you want to invest. Then we'll explain how to evaluate property for its condition and payback potential. We'll describe the type of property we call a "good" house, meaning it's in the right location and priced low enough to improve and resell at a profit. And we'll explain the formula we use to do the numbers.

Our philosophy of "flipping" a house is not buying and reselling it without taking ownership. We use the term "flip it" loosely to mean purchasing a house, *improving it*, and then reselling it. This strategy will work if you can locate and buy a house below its true market value and then make improvements that increase its value. An important piece of that puzzle is finding the right property and controlling costs while you are improving it. The faster you can turn over the property, the lower the holding costs. We see time clicking away every day we're working on a house, so it's a real incentive to complete the job and get in and get out in the shortest time possible. To help you get organized and stay focused on a project, use the worksheets in the book. They're a handy reference and overview we find useful to stay on top of a job.

Where's the Money?

One of the first decisions to make is how much money you can afford and want to invest in real estate, keeping in mind that no investment is totally risk-free. A lot depends on the economy in general, and the housing market in your area in particular, both forces you cannot control. We'll suggest how to determine your net worth and decide your debt comfort level and financing options you can leverage.

Investing in real estate introduces you to a cast of financial and housing professionals—bankers, loan officers, appraisers and home inspectors, insurance agents—and all of them will require your attention. They present you with requests for information and forms to fill out for processing, either in person or online. Approaching a lender for a mortgage on an investment property is somewhat different than a home you'll occupy, so we'll explain the difference between the types of loans and programs. We'll also give you some insight into what lenders look for when it comes to qualifying an investor.

Working with Real Estate Pros

We like working with real estate brokers for a whole lot of reasons, not the least of which is that they have access to a network of the latest listings. A good real estate broker knows all the different neighborhoods in his or her area and has connections with banks, lenders, and of course, buyers, all vital to an investor. We'll share what we've learned about working with brokers and suggest how to find one that matches your expectations. Reading a property listing sheet might seem like a no-brainer, but there are red flags to look for, so we'll explain how to read between the lines. And even though it's not as up-to-the-minute as a real-life real estate agent who calls you about a house that was just listed, we'll discuss how we use the Internet in our search for property.

Evaluating a House for Its Potential

When you're walking through a house, take a copy of our "Property Profile" in Chapter 7. This is a detailed checklist to help you inspect and evaluate the potential of every house you inspect. We admit it takes some imagination and experience to see through a neglected house that's dirty and distressed, but using the profile should help you see the Cinderella in a less-than-perfect house and focus on its potential. As the number of houses you walk through increases, they tend to blur together and it's difficult to recall the distinctions among them. So use the profiles to help you eliminate some from consideration and raise others to the top of your list.

An important part of your investment strategy revolves around whether you plan to improve a house to sell it or rent it or to live in the house for a longer period of time while you improve it. This of course depends on the condition of your house, the extent of the work required, and your time and resources. We'll walk you through the pros and cons of different strategies and suggest how they might best work for you.

Improvements and What They Cost

We've been writing about home improvements for 25 years and have seen dramatic changes in the expectations of home buyers. While a dishwasher was considered a luxury in a moderately priced home 20 years ago, today it's a necessary appliance. And a laundry room? Forget about it. All washers and dryers were down in the dark old basement. Today a laundry room is a hot button on a home buyer's wish list.

We'll discuss what adds value to a house and what doesn't. We're keen on improving certain spaces in a house like an attic, basement, and porch that are already under roof. We suggest specifics about room height, the location of stairs, and the structure itself that are key to expansion possibilities.

To know how much those improvements cost, we list the cost of all the projects you're likely to make to a house. These are dollars-and-cents figures for painting and tiling, roofing, all types of flooring, hanging everything from wallpaper to wallboard, and countless other jobs. That part of the book is an invaluable resource you'll refer to time and again.

Contractors

You need to know about hiring contractors—how to find them and how much they cost—so you'll find our best advice about working with the pros. Because hiring out labor is an important part of the equation, we look at a job and ask ourselves whether we should do the work or hire a pro. We always do the grunt work, the mindless tasks like removing wallpaper that require little in the way of tools and talents. We usually hire electricians and plumbers for rough-in work because it's required by the building inspector. We usually have floors refinished by the pros and use installers for flooring materials. We'll explain all this further in the book.

Managing a Rehab

Whether you hire a contractor to do the work or do it yourself, someone has to be in charge. A rehab is like any other production timeline, and someone has to be in control. We explain different ways to approach management and suggest you use the extensive "Checklist for Managing a Home Rehab," which you'll find very helpful. If nothing else, it's thorough and may be intimidating, but we hope you'll copy and refine it so it's a useful tool for you.

Timelines

The last three chapters of the book are timelines of houses we've worked on. We think a timeline is the best way to give you some perspective on a work in progress on three different types of rehabs. The timeline in Chapter 16 follows a fast fix-up (less than 60 days) of a ranch house that needed basic repair and cosmetic work. In Chapter 17, the six-month timeline chronicles the expansion of a two-bedroom, one-bath Cape Cod into a four-bedroom, two-bathroom home. And Chapter 18 records the challenges and rewards of a three-year plan of living in and restoring a historic home.

We hope the timelines paint a realistic picture of the process of work; naturally each house was different and our time commitment to them was too. Although different in scope and time, each of the houses turned out to be very good investments.

CHAPTER 2

PERSONALITY TRAITS FOR A SUCCESSFUL REAL ESTATE INVESTOR

The many facets of investing in real estate make it a demanding yet rewarding challenge. Of the successful career renovators we know, there are some personality traits and skills they all seem to possess. These are personality traits and skills that will see you through the ups and downs and uncertainty of finding and fixing property for a profit. There's no guarantee, but if you have most of these tendencies, we predict you're well suited for the venture.

Orderly and Well Organized

It's one thing to work on a home project with unlimited time and resources, but it's quite another to work within a time limit and budget. If you are a handy home owner who likes nothing more than spending Saturday in the basement putzing around, you might think that trait would be ideal for a rehabber. Actually, it isn't. Working on houses for resale or as rental property takes discipline, so that you waste as little time as possible. Handy or not, someone who can break a project into phases, itemize the tools and materials required, and then make one shopping expedition to buy what's needed is better suited to rehabbing houses than is a free spirit. If you have the vision to see the overall scope of a project and can break it down into compartments, you'll take a systematic approach and get the job done.

Tenacious

Anyone in sales will tell you that the most difficult but most important part of any sales job is closing the deal. Completing the transaction or finishing the job is just as important in rehabbing houses. The attractive appeal of a new paint job is lost when the walls and ceiling sparkle in contrast to the dirty old gray on the window trim and doors. A new laminate kitchen floor looks spectacular, but without the baseboard trim it's a glaring distraction. Tenacity is a personality trait that will see you through the ups and downs of working on a deadline.

Decisive and Reactive

Are you comfortable making decisions? Not everyone is. For whatever reason, making decisions can be stressful, but they can't be avoided when you're renovating property. There are just too many decisions to make—will the work on a house overimprove it for the neighborhood; should you repair or replace bathroom fixtures; what's the best color to paint the shutters? The list of decisions when bringing a house up to market value can be staggering, and often there's no time to mull them over. When you're running behind schedule and your order for kitchen cabinets is delayed, can you reassess your options and decide on a different type of cabinet that is available? As life teaches us, the best-laid plans don't always work out, and your ability to rethink options and recover from curveballs is important. If you are resourceful and can react to unexpected issues that arise, you'll take rehabbing in stride.

Managerial

There are more Indians than chiefs because many people are good worker bees but are not comfortable delegating tasks to others. When you rehab a house you'll be managing and coordinating the work of subcontractors, making appointments with inspectors, and possibly doing some of the work yourself, all of which take considerable coordination skills. It gives new meaning to the term *multitasking*. There's nothing more frustrating than watching drywallers sit on their hands while they wait for an electrician to finish installing outlet boxes or have a crew of painters arrive and wait for the drywallers to finish sanding seams. Rehabbing a house involves parsing out work to a network of trades-people, and one person has to manage and coordinate their efforts so work is completed in sequential and logical order. Even if you're retired and working on a house in your own sweet time, you'll use management skills to schedule your workload and make sure it jives with an overall schedule.

Communication-Competent

Shy and unimposing? Those qualities are admirable, but not if you're trying to find a house with potential, improve it, and bring it to market. Asking questions, following up, and nailing down issues require ongoing face-to-face, telephone, and e-mail communication skills. That contact is essential to managing a house rehab project. Taking the initiative and making contact with real estate brokers, bankers, and service personnel are key competencies. For a landlord, it's equally important to find and keep a good tenant and make arrangements to maintain the property in good working order. That dialogue is key to keeping a rehab or rental project on the mark.

Capable of Confrontation

Some of us just aren't good at conflict. We shirk away from challenging the work or competency of others because we're not comfortable in an adversarial position. The ability to confront issues and people is important, especially if you're dealing with workers or tenants. When the Dumpster you ordered isn't delivered at the expected time, your choice is between waiting it out or picking up the phone to confront the problem. If your first reaction is to call the company and ask about the delay, that initiative will help you. Opportunities for confrontation come in many forms, from no-show tradespeople or the all-powerful cable guy to potential tenants who are continually late with the rent. You'll have fewer sleepless nights if you develop the resilience to handle conflict and take confrontation in stride.

Curious and Adventurous

No, these aren't prerequisites for Outward Bound; these are personality traits that will see you through many projects of rehabbing a house. Your curiosity to understand the materials and mechanics of a house and how it works could save you a lot of money, not to mention time. When you have a broken garbage disposal, would you take it apart or call for a replacement? The adventurous and curious rehabber would disconnect its wires, unscrew the bracket, and take it apart to see how it works—might even diagnose what's wrong. A broken window elicits questions about how the glass is held in the pane (with putty), not how to buy a whole new window. The kid who annoyed everyone by asking incessant questions about why things happened just might make a very wealthy rehabber.

Physically Durable

No, you don't have to be Iron Man, but rehabbing a house can be very physical work. Even if you hire a general contractor to manage the project, you will be working overtime to supervise and inspect the work of others. You may be staying up late working on spreadsheets or getting up early to inspect a new roof. The point is, you're working extra hours, and that takes its toll if you're not in good physical shape.

If you're doing some of the work yourself, your good health and stamina is more important. The physical work and stress of manual labor is not for the weary.

Compromising

This trait is most crucial if you are doing some of the rehab work yourself and waver on being a perfectionist. It is easy to overimprove a property by not knowing when to stop. If you tend to go to extremes, you can easily invest too much time in a rehab that won't be appreciated. You can enjoy your high standard of workmanship, but don't expect someone to pay for it. Certainly the hours you spent removing all the old paint on the window will be appreciated by a tenant, but there's little guarantee that they'll pay more to live there. Shoddy workmanship is never a good investment, but try to adjust your high standards to the economic realities of real estate and find a middle ground.

Able to Laugh at Yourself and Your Situation

If you can laugh about the mistakes and miscalculations you've made, there's a good chance you can survive any situation you get yourself into. The ability to laugh and not scream or cry is most important when you're living in a fixer-upper while it's being renovated. Can you see the humor in locking yourself in the bathroom or locking yourself out of the house? There's a good chance it will happen. How about noticing drywall dust on your granola? The idea that some people are aghast at dust on their furniture and cereal with a peculiar white haze should at least tickle your funny bone.

CHAPTER 3

OUR PERSONAL "FIX-IT-AND-FLIP-IT (OR HOLD)" STORY

To be honest, we really didn't have a formal strategy when we first started working on houses. We bought a small duplex that needed a lot of tender loving care and just started to do what had to be done. Katie's mother, a widow raising five kids, had invested in real estate over the years, and Katie's sister and cousins were in the real estate business, so houses and property values were talked about occasionally. Most of those discussions went right over our heads because we were busy teaching school at the time and didn't see ourselves as budding real estate tycoons.

After a few years of fixing up our duplex, we noticed a For Sale sign that had gone up down the street. It was in front of a two-bedroom unit, smaller than the three-bedroom unit we were living in, and the unit was in a sorry state because an elderly person lived there for many years until she died. The estate wanted to sell the property quickly in "as-is" condition. We probably would not have jumped right into purchasing the property, except that we were very familiar with the duplexes and knew what had to be done because we had just finished our renovation.

We scraped together the down payment and started to work, so there was very little strategy involved. Our move into real estate was more of a knee-jerk reaction to a lot of relatives reinforcing the idea that real estate was probably a good investment.

Once, we went to see Katie's uncle, who had done very well as a real estate developer, and she asked him for advice on real estate investing.

He looked us straight in the eyes and in a deadpan voice said, "Buy low, sell high." There was a twinkle in the corner of his eye. So much for free advice, but actually you can't state the real estate game in any simpler terms.

Fixing and flipping property isn't brain surgery, but it does take a certain attitude and aptitude to develop an investment plan and hard work to execute it. Many friends and relatives questioned our nomadic lifestyle, and it certainly isn't for everyone. We learned this early on when our friends were moving from apartments to houses. We all got together to help with the moves, but we soon were three moves up on everyone, and even a case of beer was not incentive enough to bring out the troops.

Even before we decided to get into real estate full-time, our first string of two duplexes and a couple of house renovations gave us a financial stepping-stone to change careers. But these houses were not fancy—we couldn't afford fancy property. In fact, one house we fixed up was close to Chicago's O'Hare Airport, and when the wind was just right you could almost touch the planes as they came in for a landing. To make things more interesting, the railroad tracks were about a block away. We bought the house really cheap, but it had a fireplace and a pretty good layout. We lived there for a couple of years, fixed it up, and eventually put it on the market.

It took a little time to sell because of its location. One Sunday when a real estate agent was showing the house, the wind shifted to the north and the planes started to take off on "our" runway. Of course, as soon as the planes began to buzz the house, a 100-plus-car freight train began to rumble through down the tracks. We can still remember the dutiful agent and the client lip-reading as a 747 roared overhead and the train thundered on by. Surprisingly, we sold the house, and for almost full price.

Back to our first two duplexes—it was not until we had fixed up the second duplex to the point where it was in livable condition that we had to make some choices. We had two places to live, so which one should we move into? We decided to move into the smaller second unit and rent out the larger renovated unit, which we had upgraded with a new bathroom and finished basement. We knew we could get a good rent for it. Another factor influencing our decision was the tax advantage; if we decided to sell the unit we lived in, we could roll the profit into our next house.

Uncle Sam's Incentive

Even in the 1960s the tax laws favored home ownership big-time. You could roll the profit on the sale of your primary house into lowering the basis on your next house, which allowed you to delay paying taxes on the sale. We figured that because we bought the new smaller unit at such a bargain price, we could shelter the larger potential gain when we sold it if we moved there. The larger duplex would also produce a larger cash flow. This was the beginning of our "fix-it-and-flip-it" strategy. But we never got to test this because we lived in the new unit until we got it fixed up, and then, you guessed it, we bought another house, moved, and rented the house we had just fixed up.

It did not take us long to figure out that government incentives to encourage home ownership provided a tremendous business opportunity. The ability to leverage the purchase of real estate (especially single-family houses) and tax benefits at the sale are the two fundamental reasons investing in real estate can be so profitable. We go into this a bit later in the book in more detail, but simply stated, you can purchase something of value with little of your own money but get to keep the total amount of the fixed-up property's appreciation.

The current tax laws are even more favorable than when we started. Because a good portion of many Americans' wealth is in their house, the government lets them keep tax-free up to $500,000 of the profit from the house sale. There are of course some restrictions to this provision and tax laws tend to change, so check the current tax law. But unless Congress changes the law—and that is doubtful—if you live in your primary residence for two years, you can claim the exemption. So in theory you could make a $500,000 tax-free profit on your house every third year. Depending on your tax bracket, this break makes the profit 10 percent to 30 percent more valuable than the sale of another property without this advantage.

For example, $15,000 allows us to purchase a property costing $150,000 or more, depending on the loan. If the property appreciates 15 percent, let's say to $172,500, we get to keep the increase on the $150,000 value of the property, not just on the down payment. So, the $22,500 profit is almost a 50 percent return on our $15,000 investment. Of course, there are more factors to consider, like the cost of improvements and taxes, but basically the ability to leverage real estate is what makes it so profitable.

Whatever your investment plan is, consider the great tax advantage that living in an investment house affords you. By carefully planning your move to the property in your portfolio that has the most potential for appreciation and establishing residence there, you can save a bundle.

Adjusting to the Ups and Downs of the Economy

During the three decades we have invested in real estate, the economy has had its up and downs, and so has the appreciation of our investments. Through good times and bad we have been able to adjust how we approach our real estate investing to accommodate the market and develop a strategy. We started fixing up houses in the late 1960s, and the market was pretty stable until the 1973 downturn. The market softened in the Chicago area, and we decided to stay put; we had renovated a house, sold it, and traded up, so we had a nice place to live and cash flow from our previous investments. No market lasts forever, so as the economy picked up in 1975 we decided to sell our house and move on.

About that time we both felt the need to change careers, so at the end of the school year we sold our house and bought a house we thought had great potential. We took some of the profits from the sale and bought a sailboat. Instead of moving into our new "high-potential" home, we placed our stuff in the garage, rented the house, and left for a year's adventure on our sailboat.

We enjoyed a year living on our boat on the East Coast and in the Bahamas. At the same time, the market came back. When we returned, our house had appreciated almost 20 percent, something we can't take credit for; to be honest, we would have been happy if the house had held its value. The rental income covered the mortgage and taxes, so we were in a holding pattern with a nice profit. It was not a bad place to be—owning property that was paying for itself while we enjoyed some time off.

Buy the Worst House in the Best Neighborhood

If we buy a house to live in and work on over a period of time, we now choose one that offers the most potential for appreciation by being in a prized or up-and-coming neighborhood. It might be an area of town that has a highly ranked school or a neighborhood known for its large lots and tree-lined streets. It's the kind of place where people want to live because of an ambiance and character that sets it apart and makes it special.

In those neighborhoods we look for the orphan on the block, the neglected house waiting to be upgraded to the size of the other houses being transformed with additions and expansions. Ideally, the house is the smallest and least expensive on the block, so with improvements its value can only go up and become a plum property for a buyer who wants to live in that particular neighborhood.

Of course, investing in real estate is not all peachy and positive. The return on an investment, no matter what it is, reflects the amount of risk that is associated with that investment. Purchasing and fixing up houses is no exception. The game is simple to understand: if you can't make the mortgage payments the lender will come looking for its money and the property will be sold to cover the loan. As long as you pay the mortgage you get to keep the property. So the primary exposure you face is not being able to make the payments, which is the risk every home owner faces. As our property portfolio grew, so did the need for ready cash to keep the loans current.

Weathering a Decline in Housing Prices

One of the best aspects of our fix-it-and-flip-it strategy is that unless you overextend yourself you can weather market downturns. A good example of this is the market we faced in the late 1970s. Inflation went through the roof, which was great for real estate, but the interest rates followed and buyers ran for cover. The market dried up in a matter of months. Who would buy a house with mortgage rates skyrocketing? The answer is simple: *nobody*.

At about the time the market collapsed we had renovated two houses and had just put them up for sale. We had not planned on holding these properties, but the plan soon changed and we replaced the For Sale signs with For Rent signs. We had a few years' cushion on the five-year balloon interest–only loans on the houses, and the rent covered the holding costs.

When we eventually sold the houses, we made a bit less than planned because the extra holding costs ate into the profit and we had to do minor fix-ups after renting. The point here is that if you don't overextend yourself, our strategy allows you to shift from sell to rent and weather most market downturns.

Making the Most of Moving and Improving

Another key advantage to the fix-it-and-flip-it strategy is that you can get involved in the process as deeply as you want. We started as fully employed teachers working on houses in the off hours and summer months. We then decided to move into house renovation full-time and eventually moved back and forth through several career changes, but we never stopped investing in real estate.

During the cooler real estate markets, we began writing about home improvements as an offshoot of rehabbing. With every house we bought and improved we learned new skills and had a fertile supply of how-to stories. Magazine articles led to writing books and a syndicated newspaper column called "Do It Yourself . . . Or Not?"

Fixing and flipping houses allows us to choose just how involved we want to be. Sometimes we work at it full-time, buying and selling several properties in a year; at other times we use the hold or rent part of our strategy to allow us the time to work at other projects. Our approach to real estate investing is flexible enough to fit just about any lifestyle.

Today's Investment Climate Is Ripe for Rehabbing

When we first started fixing up houses, the mortgage rates were above 6 percent. Today, some 30 years later, it's hard to believe that rates are substantially below that level and hit historic lows every day. A recent report, *The State of the Nation's Housing: 2003*, from Harvard University's Joint Center for Housing Studies, suggests a strong decade ahead for housing despite the lackluster economy. "Despite the 2001 recession and weak ensuing recovery, by most measures 2002 was the strongest year for housing on record. Residential investment, home sales, home ownership rates, and aggregate home and total mortgage debt all hit new highs last year," according to the study.

We remain confident there will always be a market for a good house. You may decide you want to concentrate on a specific type of property, build a portfolio of rental units, or invest in commercial property. Whatever your goals are, single-family residential real estate is a good place to start. As we explained at the start of this chapter, what we do is not brain surgery and the lessons we learned are worth sharing. Our plan is not a get-rich-quick scheme but a commonsense approach that allows just about anyone to participate in one of the greatest investment opportunities available anywhere in the world.

There's another perk that we've enjoyed in rehabbing houses, and we see it when we drive by the houses we've owned and improved. We like seeing that the houses are being lived in and enjoyed by families. Some look exactly as they did when we left them; others have been expanded and improved further. All of the houses have stood the test of time. And that little house near O'Hare Airport with the railroad track that almost runs through it—it's still as cute as a button. On our last drive-by we saw that the aluminum siding we installed still looks good, there's a well-used swing set in the backyard, and the smoke that was coming out of the fireplace chimney tells us the family living there enjoys the fireplace as much as we did.

CHAPTER 4

LIVING IN A FIXER-UPPER: IS IT WORTH IT? WHAT'S IT LIKE?

Is living "under construction" worth the hassles and inconveniences? Only you can decide, but it's always worked for us through various stages of our lives, whether we were a young married couple teaching school, self-employed writers and entrepreneurs, employees of a large corporation, or a couple phasing into semiretirement.

Our first properties were small and we learned by doing, either tackling home-improvement projects ourselves or looking over the shoulder of the plumber or electrician we hired. When we had stopped teaching and were working on houses full-time, we usually had our permanent residence in the process of renovation and a project house under way. Yes, it could get very complicated and unsettling at times, but as long as we had a few rooms that were complete and livable, we seemed to take it in stride.

In retrospect, we were often more concerned about the condition and storage of our tools and equipment, which became considerable as we worked on houses full-time. A garage became a key feature when we looked at houses to occupy, because we needed a safe, dry storage space for the tools and gear we were accumulating.

Kids Are a Real Concern

Living with children in a house under construction is another issue completely. It can be daunting and even dangerous when little ones are scampering around unfinished floors and playing in less-than-ideal circumstances. And of course, there are real dangers of lead poisoning and asbestos in an older house being remodeled.

The Environmental Protection Agency has a pamphlet called *Protect Your Family from Lead in Your Home* and others available through the National Lead Information Clearinghouse (800-424-LEAD). Their website, epa.gov, includes information about asbestos in the home, where it may be found, and what should be done about it. If you're considering a major rehab and have children, do some research before you make a decision.

All children and most adults appreciate structure in their lives, and the unpredictable nature of rehabbing can be very stressful. If rehabbing takes you from one house to another, consider the effects on kids changing schools—this can be unsettling. Many families get around this by narrowing their scope of investment properties to houses within a particular school district so their kids don't have to change schools.

A Second Job

We think of a house that we live in and work on as a second job that costs us money in the short term but in the long run generates a substantial profit. It provides a place to hang our hats (and store our tools) and at the same time requires either our time or our money or both. But if we choose the property wisely and improve it with care, our investment will pay off. That's true for a single owner or two married wage earners who have full-time jobs that can support the costs of improvements as they are required.

If you're considering buying to renovate a house but are strapped for time, consider buying the house with a longer-term plan and let the value of the property rise over time. When writing about home improvements led us to building an online business, we stayed where we were and turned all our time and energy to the business instead of completing the house and buying another one. We converted bedrooms to workstations and worked at home until we found an office, all the while letting the home slowly grow in value.

If the economy is strong, that's a strategy that works, but if your job forces you to move, you're vulnerable and may have to sell during a downturn—not a good position to be in. Experience has taught us that you're in control if you don't have to sell and can wait out adverse conditions so you can take advantage of a sellers' market.

Prioritizing Improvements with a Plan

The best approach to living in a fixer-upper is to create a twofold plan. Start with a long-range plan for completing the house to its ultimate condition with a working estimate of the investment dollars you plan to spend on the house. That's the overall plan and budget to upgrade the property. (For specific plans and timelines, see the last chapters in this book.)

Make a short-term plan that's more immediate. It should include quick fixes and repairs to make the house safe. Take care of a faulty roof, plumbing, heating, and other essential elements of the house. Then make low-cost instant-gratification improvements that you can enjoy while living there. We always paint the rooms and refinish hardwood floors to create a clean new living environment. No matter what the ultimate decorating scheme is, we start with a coat of white paint on the walls that freshens the look and gives it a nice clean smell, and we add inexpensive miniblinds to the windows. Other quick fixes can be things like repairing a wobbly railing on the back stairs, replacing the handle on a sliding patio door, adding a new mailbox, painting the front door— any improvements that are necessary to make it more functional and attractive.

If a house doesn't have a shower—which tops our priority list of creature comforts—we have a plumber run the lines and valves for a new shower but leave the rest of the room as is until we're ready to remodel it.

In one house there was no storage space to speak of, but there was an unfinished attic, so before we did anything else we built pull-down attic stairs to give us access to the space. In many bedroom closets of older homes we replaced the traditional "one shelf" with shelving components that greatly increased the storage capacity. These inexpensive improvements increased the livability of a house, and we could enjoy them immediately.

Sometimes the first improvements are not cosmetic—such as upgrades to the heating and cooling or electrical systems. Both are often required in houses without air-conditioning or enough outlets.

We put off any improvements that change the floor plan of a house until after we've lived there because it's important to see how it works. Moving a wall might seem like a good idea, but until you've lived in a space to see how it functions, it's difficult to consider all the choices you have. While it doesn't seem so at the time, there are advantages to living in a kitchen and understanding its shortcomings before tearing it apart. Only by living in a house can you see how the windows in a room open up the space to daylight or recognize the need to widen the window opening to a family room.

Coping Strategies for Daily Life in a Fixer-Upper

If you like to camp, you'll love to live in a fixer-upper because sometimes you are reduced to that level of preparing food or using a tiny bathroom or other conditions that are temporarily out of your control. It's not always the case, but it's better to expect a worst-case scenario than to imagine that rehabbing your kitchen won't really change your life. It will. Planning and preparation, of course, can make it bearable, but when you tear apart the center of your household, it's going to affect everyone until it's all put back together.

Don't be surprised when the ongoing activity of contractors and inspectors moving through your home makes some family members cranky. It can be very stressful. Decide on an area of the house or some rooms that will be off-limits to those who are not members of the family. Many people undergoing a rehab project need an oasis that's removed from the day-to-day commotion.

We should emphasize that everyone in a household is affected when your house is in a work zone, including your pets. Don't be surprised if your favorite feline doesn't like the idea of change. And Fido just might not adjust well to the noise and confusion of a major rehab, let alone welcome workers inside. The only bright spot for our pets was their enjoyment of smelling, licking, and discovering new openings for windows and doors and following new heat ducts through attic floor joists.

We always had trouble finding Pete and Repete, our cats, when the second floor of one of our houses was under construction. They'd find clever ways to squirrel into floor cavities and hide behind wall partitions that kept us searching for them. Once, the only way to lure Pete out of a floor joist was with the Thanksgiving turkey. The smell is what got him. The point is that you're upsetting all the members of your household—not just the humans—when you change the structure of your house and your daily routines and lifestyle.

When a Kitchen Undergoes a Major Overhaul

- Pare down items in kitchen cabinets to the bare minimum.
- Make temporary countertops with sheets of plywood so you have some work surfaces.
- Create a makeshift kitchen with a refrigerator on the back porch or in the basement. Set up a microwave and buy microwave entrées, eat out, or get carry-home meals. Use paper plates so you have to wash only silverware and glasses.
- Set up an inexpensive metal cabinet to store essentials in the kitchen or near it.
- Keep a shop vacuum handy so it's easy to clean up after workers (if they don't).

When a Bathroom Gets a Makeover

- If it's the only bathroom in the house, carefully schedule the work so there's always a toilet that works and a shower for bathing.
- Double-check the materials (floor tile, fixtures, et cetera) when they arrive to make sure they are what was ordered.
- Make sure there's always one electrical outlet to power hair dryers, electric shavers, and so on.
- Coordinate family members' bathroom time and keep it to a minimum (well, try anyway).

Getting Used to an Open-Door Policy

- Be prepared for an ongoing trail of workers and inspectors, and keep a log of the days and times of their visits. Also make note of what was discussed, determined, or agreed on with any action on your part.
- Keep a folder, basket, or other container for receipts of deliveries that come into the house. You can file them away in the proper place at a later date, but it eliminates the search for them at this point in the renovation.
- Designate one area—a garage is ideal—to store all the materials that come into the house for a project. Open all materials when they arrive, check that the size, style, and number are correct, and note their condition.

Seeing the Positive Side of a Renovation

Don't get the idea that rehabbing has only a dark side. We wouldn't have done it for so long if it were that miserable. There are many bright sides to bohemian living. For one, you have an ongoing excuse to keep things simple, which is especially handy when you're entertaining. Rehabbing is also reason enough to lower your standards for a clean house. It's the perfect excuse, actually. In its place, however, keeping the stuff in the house orderly is much more important. On another plane, it helps you prioritize what's really important to you and your family. We found the challenge of planning a project, completing it, and enjoying the results was very satisfying.

The relaxed lifestyle calls for taking advantage of the situation. For example, when we removed all the plaster walls in the second floor of one house and exposed wall studs and framing, we used them as clothes hangers. When we needed a place to hang a pair of jeans or sweats, we'd bang a heavy nail into the stud and—voilà—instant clothes hook. Nothing could be simpler. At the time we were writing a series about remodeling for the *Washington Post Home Section* and were amazed to hear from many readers embarked on the same rehabbing adventure.

We had friends who let their kids use the walls in one bedroom as a giant canvas because the walls were coming down to become part of a kitchen family room. They used markers, paint, and crayons, and it became a favorite game room for all the kids in the neighborhood.

We found living in a house under construction to be appealing and practical, but it's not for everyone. It was our idea of double dipping: you have a place to live while you are working on improving the property. If you are contemplating this approach, we suggest you go to a video store and rent the movie *Money Pit*. It is a comedy, but the movie brings to light, in a glamorized and exaggerated form, some of the realities of living in a work zone. If you watch the video and everyone involved still buys into the idea, you're ready to move ahead!

CHAPTER 5

TAILORING A FIX-UP STRATEGY TO FIT YOUR LIFESTYLE

R ehabbing a house for resale or rent is nothing less than a second job, but there are ways to pull it off on flextime. This chapter is a reality check on the amount of time and resources the project requires. You have probably already heard the old saying "Time is money." This cliché is certainly quoted by businesspeople, especially in the construction industry. Before you consider jumping headfirst into rehabbing a property, take time to formulate a plan that you and your family can realistically fit into your lives. Any venture outside of your regular employment, including investing in real estate, will require changes in everyone's lifestyle.

Choosing a Strategy That Works for You

There are several approaches you can take to tackling this challenge. If your present job and family obligations allow you little extra time, your best plan may be to buy, improve, and rent a small property. If, on the other hand, you think you can carve out the time and energy from your existing lifestyle and focus it on a renovation, a quick-turnover strategy may work better for you. It's called creative thinking. If you are willing to put forth the effort, you can develop a strategy to purchase, rehab, and then sell or hold a property, whatever your situation.

Fast Return on Your Money

To most real estate professionals the term "flip it" means buying and reselling a property without actually taking possession of it. Of course you can't actually fix it if you technically flip it, so in the context of *Fix It and Flip It*, we use the term "flip it" loosely to mean purchasing a house, *improving* it, and then reselling it. This strategy works if you can locate and purchase property below its true market value and then rehab it to increase its value to at least market value or more.

The key to making this strategy work is not only finding the right property but controlling costs while you are improving it. So the faster you can turn over the property, the lower the holding costs will be. As long as you hold title to the property, the clock is ticking; and each tick increases the cost of taxes, insurance, interest, and utilities. For example, in winter to keep the pipes from freezing, you will have to heat the property, which in a large or older house can add up fast.

Of course, this cost should be figured into your renovation budget, but if you can get the project completed ahead of schedule it's money in your pocket. And should the project drag on and on, the holding cost will take a big bite out of any projected profits.

To be successful at a quick turnover you must be able to juggle the requirements to get the job done and control costs. You must carefully weigh the possible savings of doing some or most of the renovation yourself against subcontracting the work out. Many times professionals can complete the project faster, especially if you have other demands on your time. The fast-turnover strategy may also require additional working capital because the cost of property and its renovation will be compressed into a short time.

Gimme Shelter: Renovate to Occupy

One of the best advantages of investing in real estate is that your investment can provide you shelter while you improve it and wait for another good property to come on the market. In the mid-1960s we purchased our first property, a run-down duplex in suburban Chicago. The unit was basically sound but needed lots of TLC. We worked at painting the interior, renovating the kitchen, installing carpeting, and transforming the basement into a family room while we lived in the unit. This took several years to complete.

At that time we both held full-time jobs and didn't have the time or want to make the time to devote to a fast turnover. Eventually another duplex came on the market in the same neighborhood and we bought it, found a tenant for our first unit, moved into the new building, and started all over. We had our first property producing a positive cash flow while we were working on the next.

Another advantage to this strategy is that you can get a better financing deal. Lenders require a much smaller down payment if you occupy the property, which can reduce the amount of investment capital you require. Down payments of less than 5 percent are not uncommon for owner-occupied properties. If you live in the property when you sell, you get a tax break because it is your primary residence.

Renovate to Rent

When you plan to rent out the property instead of occupying it yourself, of course the holding cost clock is still ticking before the property begins to earn a return. But because you plan to hold the property for a longer period of time, the holding cost is spread over this time.

This strategy is a good fallback if the market should change while you are in the middle of a renovation. In the late '70s, the interest rates went up like a skyrocket, and the housing market came to a screeching halt just as we had a property ready for market. It was obvious that the house would take a while to sell, so we quickly found a tenant because the house was in move-in condition. For the next couple of years the rent covered our holding costs and eventually the market came back. The house actually appreciated a bit, and we were able to sell it for more than our target selling price. In addition, the rent paid off a small portion of the mortgage.

Looking at Choices: Adjusting Your Lifestyle to Rehabbing a House

Investing in real estate can be rewarding both financially and emotionally. Breathing new life into a rundown house is rewarding in itself, but the satisfaction of having your efforts appreciated by a new buyer is very gratifying and can be profitable. But like many things in life, rehabbing a house—even a small one—will be close to a full-time job. Even if you plan to subcontract most of the actual construction, you or a partner will have to plan and supervise the project.

Before you look for your first property, make a basic decision about the time commitment and the size of the investment you can make. Any of the strategies can make you money; the idea is to take the approach that works best for you. And who knows, even with the best-laid plans, you may find yourself switching from one to another as circumstances change.

To help you decide on an investment strategy, spend some time considering how it will change your life as you know it. That sounds a bit lofty, but your life will change and so will your priorities. It's true that planning is half the fun, but in the property-renovation business, planning and contingency planning are everything. Here are some topics to consider as you create your overall investment strategy.

Job Considerations

We are assuming that most of you soon-to-be real estate tycoons are now employed doing something other than fixing and flipping houses. When we started to work on our early properties, we were fully employed schoolteachers. This type of work was demanding and the school day was full, but we did not have long commutes and we had most evenings and weekends off. The schedule allowed us to work on our first property for about 20 hours a week without killing ourselves. Sometimes we had to really press on into the night to get projects like the kitchen and bath completed because we needed them operational as soon as possible. We also had holidays and two months off during the summer—the ideal time for us to purchase a property. Sometimes we were fortunate to find a property to close on in June and work like mad during the summer to get it back on the market in the fall. Sometimes we didn't. The "renovate to occupy" strategy worked for us because we had the luxury of free time and we had the experience from our early investments.

Make a careful assessment of your present job and how much spare time you can devote to a real estate project. It's important that your time estimates err on the conservative side because it's better to finish a project earlier than anticipated than later. But don't be discouraged if the timing of your first house rehab project isn't right on. Scheduling work is a fine art, and without any previous experience it's difficult to plan far into the future. If you are a neophyte like we were, you will most likely learn that your first estimates will need revising.

Retired and Ready to Work

Retired empty nesters are foraging the country for investment opportunities because they have the time, the money, and the skills to transform property. Many are looking for a house project as a sort of part-time job; others want investment property as a bridge job before they retire. They are stiff competition for worker bees with busy family lives who are looking for the same thing.

A key advantage retirees have over first-time working investors is their gray hair, which counts for wisdom when it comes to buying and selling houses. No kidding. Most people have bought and sold houses through their working years as their family and income have grown. Those years of owning and maintaining a house translate to well-heeled experience. Retirees make up a growing number of seasoned rehabbers who have the hindsight and skills to either manage the renovation of a house or the time to do some or all of the work.

Relationships

Probably more important than your job is assessing your family relationships. Even if you are single, relationships take time to maintain. Managing a renovation project is time-consuming, and doing the work yourself can be downright backbreaking. Little League, that weekly golf game, and most social events take time away from an investment property. We're not suggesting you have to resign from the human race to fix and flip a house, but you have to be realistic about how you spend your time. For some investors, fixing and flipping a house is their full-time hobby.

If you share your time with a spouse or significant other, is he or she willing to give that time up while you spend free time and weekends at an investment property? Is your partner willing to devote his or her own time to the project? If so, how much? At the risk of this sounding like marriage counseling, we've got to tell you that rehabbing a house can put a tremendous strain on a relationship. Years ago we wrote an article for *Home* magazine called "Coping with a Handyman Special," and we got an earful when we interviewed marriage counselors. The bottom line was that the issues of time and money were hot buttons between couples arguing about a house they bought without enough time and money to see them through the project. Talk it out, work it out, and nail down the time and money you're both willing to invest before jumping in.

Up-Front Time Commitment

One of the greatest challenges you will face in your real estate investment career is finding the right properties to buy and improve and be profitable. The operative word here is *profitable*. Unless you live in a very sparsely populated part of the country, there are literally dozens of properties available for sale that need work. Some offer opportunity, but many are not suitable for fixing and flipping.

Searching for property while you establish a network of real estate brokers takes time. This can be fun; just be aware that looking at and analyzing properties will soak up a lot of time before you find the right project. Then as you get one property ready for market, you should be on the lookout for another one. In fact, the search should never stop even while you are up to your neck in a project.

Learn the Time-Allocation Dance

As we indicated at the beginning of this chapter, you must weigh your time against your money. But the equation is not as simple as that.

Sometimes your time is worth more doing things other than painting or hanging wallboard, sometimes not. Be realistic about your skill set.

You may be a great salesperson or computer programmer and a downright lousy carpenter. That doesn't necessarily mean you can't fix and flip property. It does mean you are probably better off working a little overtime and putting that extra cash toward subcontracting the carpentry. The point is, if you have a job that pays overtime or gives extra compensation for extra work, you could be better off working on a Saturday or during evenings and farming out some of the rehab work instead of doing the work yourself.

However you decide to budget your time, your involvement in managing the project will be the most valuable. You've created a plan to purchase a property, have made plans to improve it, and have determined your budget—these are all management skills, key ingredients for an investor. But in your planning stages consider that supervision of the work is costly when you hire someone to do it. If you have the skills, you may have a hard time justifying paying a general contractor 10 to 15 percent to do it. On the other hand, until you get experience, a large rehab involving extensive remodeling and possible structural changes might be better served by professional management. Until you establish a working relationship with reliable subcontractors, a general contractor may be able to get the work done faster and in some cases cheaper. In Chapter 14, "Who Does the Work? Who Manages the Job?" we discuss this in greater detail.

CHAPTER 6

FINDING THE MONEY

It is our experience that investing in real estate requires some ready cash and decent credit. We do not give "get-rich-quick-in-real-estate" seminars and have not used the no-money-down techniques to purchase real estate. We do it the old-fashioned way—we earn it. Sorry to disappoint—if you're looking for a financial-freedom seminar, we can't offer any advice on making money without working for it. What fits our style of investing is to develop solid relationships with commercial banks and savings and loan associations and carefully use consumer credit.

When we started investing, banks and savings and loans were much more conservative with lending practices. Most required at least 20 percent of the cost of the property as a down payment. Many lenders were reluctant to even make loans on property that was not owner occupied. Fortunately for us, we lived in our first couple of properties so the financing was easier to acquire, but we still had to put 20 percent down.

What many investors say about banks is true: banks are more eager to lend you money when you don't need it than when you do. And we found it to be true. After working with several commercial banks and savings and loans on our first properties, we established a good track record and the institutions soon began to look at us as valued customers.

Real Estate as an Investment

Like any business, buying property, improving it, and then selling or renting it requires working capital. How much working capital depends on your creativity and resourcefulness, as well as on the scope of your project. One of the first steps to take is to decide how much you can afford to invest and want to invest in real estate. No investing is totally risk-free, and that's true for investing in real estate. As with other forms of investing, the more risk you are willing to take, the higher the potential reward.

Purchasing a property, improving it, and selling it for a profit depends on market forces that, for the most part, are beyond your control. A property that seems like a sure thing in a hot market may not pan out six or eight months later. Real estate is also less liquid than many other investments; you have to sell the property, trade it, or refinance it to realize the gain. Can you afford to wait out a down market? Your strategy should take this into account.

On the other hand, real estate ownership gives you a tangible asset, a house to live in, a rental property, or a vacant lot. Given enough time, real estate has historically appreciated in value. City neighborhoods go in and out of favor. Some of the worst were once the best and given time, will probably become desirable again. We paid less than $16,000 for our first duplex and were happy to sell it five years later for more than $28,000. That's a pretty good return on our original $3,200 investment. Today, some 25 years later, it is selling for $185,000.

Timing is a large factor in real estate investing. In addition to asking yourself how much you can afford to invest, look at how long the money can be tied up. Depending on your strategy, your money could be tied up for a year or so on a fix it and flip it or for several years in a renovate-to-rent or renovate-to-occupy scenario. Funds that will be needed in the near future, like those for children's education, are best placed in a more liquid investment—unless the children are toddlers, and then there's plenty of time for property to appreciate.

Get Your Financial House in Order

Take the time to make an honest assessment of your net worth and determine how much hard cash you can commit to investing in real estate. Even if you are going to try a no-money-down strategy (you didn't hear it from us), the seller will want to know something about your financial condition. Be prepared to bare your financial soul to the lenders. To determine how much capital you have to invest in real estate, gather together your financial records and get things in order. (Everyone should do this once a year, whether they're investing or not.)

You get an A+ if all you have to do is go to your personal computer and ask Quicken or Microsoft Money for a net worth report. If you have to plow through records and stacks of statements and commit your findings to paper, consider buying a financial-management software program. Lending officers appreciate receiving a nicely formatted financial report, and the presentation tells them you have a handle on your affairs. Financial-management software is essential to keeping you in control of expenses as you get into real estate investing.

The low-tech way to determine your net worth is basic accounting. Take a piece of paper and draw a line down the center to form two columns. In the left-hand column list the value of the assets you have. Include everything you can think of, such as savings accounts, insurance, cars, market value of your house, investments, and retirement accounts such as IRAs and 401(k)s. In the right-hand column list all your debts, including mortgages, credit cards, car loans, personal loans, and outstanding bills.

Subtract the right column from the left and you have a good idea of your net worth. You may be surprised at the figure—pleasantly surprised or disappointed; either way, it gives you a realistic picture of your financial condition at this point in time.

What Lenders Look For

When you apply for credit, lenders check for certain criteria. Here is an overview of what they look at:

Credit Report

Your credit report shows the lender what kind of borrower you are, how much you owe, whether you pay on time, and if you have had any bankruptcies, judgments, repossessions, or delinquent accounts. Your credit report is actually a credit history. It is created by data about you from many different sources. Companies that have granted you credit make regular reports about your accounts to the three main credit reporting agencies. A good credit history allows the lender to offer you a larger loan at a better interest rate. On the other hand, a low credit score means the lender may offset the risk by reducing the loan to value and raising the interest rate.

Getting Your Credit Report

Ordering your credit report once a year and knowing your credit reporting rights are important steps to safeguarding your privacy. You can obtain a copy of your report by writing or calling one of the three credit reporting agencies (CRAs). Ordinarily the charge is less than $10 unless you live in Colorado, Georgia, Maryland, Massachusetts, New Jersey, or New York, where there is no charge.

For a copy of your report write, call, or connect online with the CRAs:

Equifax, Inc.
P.O. Box 740241
Atlanta, GA 30374
800-685-1111
equifax.com

Experian, National Consumer Assistance
P.O. Box 2104
Allen, TX 75013-2104
888-397-3742
experian.com

Trans Union LLC, Consumer Disclosure Center
P.O. Box 1000
Chester, PA 19022
800-888-4213
transunion.com

To get a copy of your report you will have to give the CRA the following information:

- Full name
- Social security number
- Driver's license information
- Current address and your addresses within the past five years
- Date of birth
- Signature
- Home telephone number
- Employer

Income and Home Equity

Your income and length of time at work are factors taken into account in qualifying for a loan. Most lenders like to see a minimum of two years in the same job or the same type of work. The income used in determining your creditworthiness depends on the source. Salary or wages are always counted directly, while overtime or bonuses will be averaged for the past year or two. For self-employed borrowers, the net income is averaged for the past two years. Other income may or may not be included.

The home equity loan debt ratio has two parts: the total housing expense divided by the total income, and the total of all debts divided by the total income. The more equity you have, the lower the perceived risk to the lender. The percentage of equity relative to the value of your home is an important factor for loan approval and the rate of interest.

Building Collateral

To raise the balance of the money you can invest in real estate, take a look at your list of assets to see if any can be converted into cash. You may not have to sell a well-established art collection to convert it into cash, but it can be used as collateral to secure a loan. Besides taking money out of savings, here are some traditional methods you can use to generate cash:

Refinancing

If you own a house and its value is substantially above the mortgage balance, you can free up the equity by refinancing. This is especially true when interest rates are low, but no matter where the interest rates happen to fall, if you have equity in your house you can apply for a new larger mortgage.

For example, you may have an existing mortgage with a balance of $75,000. If your house has appreciated to a market value of $150,000, you can refinance it with a conventional 10 percent owner-occupied mortgage and free up $50,000 to $60,000. Basically the bank will make a mortgage for 90 percent of the house's value. The new mortgage will be $135,000, and from these funds the balance of the old mortgage is paid off. The length of your new mortgage can be increased from 20 to 30 years to keep down the size of the payments. However convenient this may be, remember you are taking on debt that must be repaid and you are living on the collateral.

Second Mortgage

Another method to free up equity in a house is to take out a second mortgage. Most lenders will take a second mortgage on a house even if you have little or no equity in the property. If you have good credit you can get a loan for up to 125 percent of the house's value. The main advantage of a second mortgage is the low rate relative to other financing.

The most common type of second mortgage is a fixed-rate, simple-interest loan, and it does not change the terms of the current first mortgage. The interest portion of a second mortgage can be tax-deductible.

Home Equity Loan

A home equity loan makes sense especially if you already have a low interest rate on your first mortgage. Most lenders offer flexible loan guidelines that allow a home equity loan to be used to pay off debts, make home improvements, or choose a combination with a personal cash out.

Many lenders do not require home equity for a new loan, with programs available up to 100 percent or more of the value of your house. Terms can range from five to 30 years. The tax savings can be substantial when compared to nondeductible debt. Check with your tax adviser for current details.

Home Equity Credit Line

A home equity credit line is a revolving credit line account secured by the equity in your home. This type of loan has a variable interest rate based on the prime rate. The loan can be active for a long period, typically 10 to 15 years. During this period, you have the option of making interest-only payments or regular amortized payments. At the end of the line of credit period, the existing balance may be converted to a standard loan.

The major difference between a home equity credit line and a home equity loan is that with a credit line, you withdraw funds only as needed. For example, the line of credit may be for $50,000, but you need only $20,000 for a down payment on an investment property. You draw on the line of credit for only $20,000 and pay interest only on the actual amount you use.

Many lenders will extend a credit line of up to 100 percent of the value of your house. A home equity credit line is available for owner-occupied single-family homes, condominiums, and townhouses. Because an equity credit line is secured by your primary home, the interest may be tax deductible.

Sell Your House and Downsize

Another method to realize the equity built up in your home is to sell it and purchase a less valuable property. The funds are tax sheltered, and you will save the interest you have to pay on borrowed funds. This method allows you to get investment capital without having to use your house as collateral. Any business venture has some risk involved, but using this technique you are assured of a roof over your head as long as you pay your mortgage.

Borrow Against Your Assets

Banks will make loans secured by other types of assets such as cars, boats, jewelry, and collections, which can be used to secure a loan. Of course, the lender must consider the asset valuable enough. In some cases the collateral can be used to secure a portion of a personal loan, allowing the lender to make a larger loan than they would based on your signature alone.

Personal Loan

People with good credit may be able to secure a personal loan without having to pledge assets as collateral. Unless the borrower has considerable personal wealth and a good relationship with the lender, few institutions will lend large sums of money secured by a signature only.

Family, friends, and business associates may be willing to make a personal loan, which may be a good source for a small amount to put the finishing touches on a property—for example, if your equity line of credit is several thousand dollars short and a quick $5,000 loan from a relative will give you the capital to complete a house and get a For Rent sign on the front lawn.

Set Your Budget

Before we look at the different financing options available to you as a real estate investor, decide the dollar amount you can afford to invest and are comfortable risking. If you already have property, you have to decide how much you want to earmark for real estate.

Using debt to buy consumer goods such as a TV or car produces no return because those items depreciate in value. But borrowing funds to purchase assets such as real estate that can increase in value has been used for centuries and is the basis of many large fortunes. Debt allows you to leverage the funds you have to increase your return on investment.

An important point to remember in deciding your debt comfort level is that debt, if used wisely, is good. One of the best aspects of real estate investing is that you enter the business at any level where you feel comfortable. Our first properties were very modest duplexes that we lived in, so we were able to secure favorable financing. The average cost of a single-family home in the United States is around $150,000. Using an owner-occupied 90 percent mortgage, you could purchase the property for less than $15,000. A modest renovation might call for $8,000 in repairs, so basically a budget of about $25,000 is needed.

As the cost of property goes up, the initial capital needed to purchase and renovate it also rises. The main point to remember is that if you purchase the property right and make the correct improvements, your rate of return will be good for any level of investment. Starting small does not mean you have to stay small.

Whatever amount you decide to invest, don't commit the total amount to any one project. Always reserve funds to cover unexpected expenditures. Renovating any house, and particularly an old one, holds some surprises; by maintaining a contingency fund you will be sure to have the funds to cover the unexpected.

Use Other People's Money

When you decide how much you want to begin investing, the next step is to look at sources of additional financing to leverage that investment. Remember that the ability to use other sources of money to purchase real estate is one of its most compelling aspects. Leverage is the ability to purchase a property with borrowed funds and increase the rate of return of the money you actually invest. For example, if you plan to live in a house you can get a mortgage for 90 percent of its appraised value. On a $200,000 house, you will invest $20,000 and the bank will put up the other 90 percent. Ignoring expenses, if over the next three years the property appreciates 10 percent you could sell it for $220,000 and realize $40,000 in cash from the sale after you paid off the $180,000 mortgage. The $40,000 difference represents a 100 percent return on your original $20,000 investment. If you paid cash for the house you would have made a $20,000 profit on a $200,000 investment, a nice 10 percent return but nowhere near the leveraged deal.

Of course, just as leverage works to increase your rate of return, it can increase your losses. Should the value of the property decline 10 percent or more you could find yourself in a situation where the property's sale won't generate enough cash to pay off the mortgage. Not only would you lose your initial $20,000 investment, you would also owe the bank the difference between the mortgage balance and the sale price of the property.

Even in that scenario, as long as you make the mortgage payments you don't have to sell the property. Markets move up and down, but historically real estate values in the United States continue to rise over time. The ability to change investment strategies to reflect market conditions can lessen the risk that highly leveraged properties can present. Changing from a fix-it-and-flip-it strategy to a fix-it-and-rent-it or fix-it-and-occupy-it strategy could allow you to weather a potential downturn.

Financing Options

Securing financing is one of the most important aspects of real estate investing. Without a source of borrowed money, the leveraging advantages are lost. There are many financing options available to anyone with good credit and a decent employment record. We will begin at the least expensive (lowest interest rate) options and work down the list.

Owner-Occupied Financing

As long as you initially plan to live in the property you qualify for owner-occupied financing. With this type of financing the lender expects you to move into the property. It's not unusual for people to move because borrowers' situations change, so mortgages are honored by lenders as long as the payments are made.

Just how long you have to live in the house is a tricky question. Most lenders do not check on occupancy once the loan has closed; they rely on your trustworthiness. Moving in, working on the property, and then moving on in a year or so would probably not upset the apple cart. You do want to maintain a relationship with the lender, so if you are going to use owner-occupied financing to get a better interest rate and lower down payment, plan to spend at least a year in the property.

Fixed-Rate Loan

A conventional fixed-rate mortgage offers you a set rate and payments that do not change throughout the life of the loan. A conventional loan is paid off over a given number of years, usually 15, 20, or 30. A portion of each monthly payment goes toward the principal, and the rest is interest. Most lenders roll the cost of insurance and taxes into the monthly payment.

Adjustable-Rate Loan

An adjustable-rate mortgage (ARM) has a fluctuating interest rate. In most ARM mortgages, the interest rate is fixed for a certain number of years and then allowed to move up or down in sync with current economic conditions. The flexible interest rate lowers the risk for the lender, and in exchange they offer a lower initial interest rate.

The three most important factors to consider when applying for an ARM are the adjustment period, the interest cap, and the index used to calculate the interest. The adjustment period consists of two parts: the length of time before the bank can adjust the rate, and after that period, how often the bank may adjust the rate.

The cap is the limit to individual and cumulative interest-rate adjustments. The cap has two parts: the first is the total amount of interest the bank can raise the loan in any given period, and the second is the total amount the bank can raise the interest rate. For example, an ARM could have a 3 percent step limit with a 6 percent total. This will prevent the bank from raising the interest more than 3 percent in any step and puts a limit to the total interest rate increase to 6 percent. A 5.5 percent ARM could not rise above 11.5 percent or go up more than 3 percent at any step.

The rate of the ARM is usually tied to some index or the prime rate. It is usually expressed as the interest rate you will pay for the fixed period of the loan and then the index, plus some additional rate that the adjustable rate is calculated from. For example, the index may be the prime rate plus 3 percent. In the case where the prime rate is 5 percent at the time of adjustment, the loan rate would be adjusted to 8 percent. If the prime were 6.5 percent, the loan would be adjusted to 8.5 percent because there is a cap of 3 percent per step.

Balloon Loans

A conventional, fixed-rate mortgage with a term that is much shorter than the terms of the payments is called a balloon loan. For example, a mortgage with a payment schedule for a 30-year loan with a due date of three years is a balloon loan. This type of loan allows the bank to loan money at a fixed lower rate because the duration of the loan is short.

We found that this type of financing works well with a fix-it-and-flip-it strategy. The plan is to purchase and renovate the property and then sell it. The balloon loan can be structured to provide ample time for the renovation, but the short term gives more security to the lending institution.

In addition to a low monthly payment that a 30-year payment schedule gives, many lenders are willing to make this an interest-only loan because the actual equity payments during the three-year balloon period are small. At the end of the balloon period you must refinance the loan if the property is not sold.

Low-Down-Payment Programs

Many lenders offer loans that require little if any down payment. This type of loan will allow you to get the most leverage when purchasing a property.

5 Percent Down Conventional Loan

- Most lenders will make this loan if you have good credit and adequate income.
- All loans are fixed-rate loans.

3 Percent Down Conventional Loan

- Most lenders will make this loan if you have good credit and adequate income.
- All loans are fixed-rate loans.

No-Down-Payment Loans

These types of loans, designed for first-time home buyers, make it affordable to buy a home you can qualify for and live in.

103 Percent Loan to Value, Zero Down Plus

- Mortgage up to 100 percent of the purchase price.
- Closing costs may be financed up to an additional 3 percent.
- Good credit is required.
- These are usually available on 15- and 30-year fixed-rate programs.

80/20 (80 Percent First Mortgage Plus a 20 Percent Second Mortgage)

- No down payment is required.
- These are available on 15- and 30-year fixed-rate programs.

Investor Nonoccupied Financing

Getting financing for investor property to fix up or rent is more difficult than for owner-occupied property. Banks will usually not finance more than 75 percent of the appraised value of the property, and the property must be able to generate sufficient cash to repay the loan.

Land Contracts

Land contracts-of-sale have been used for decades as a way to transfer title to a property when the buyer does not have enough money to purchase the property outright. A land contract-of-sale is a purchase contract where the seller holds the deed until the full selling price is received. Terms of payment are agreed upon between seller and purchaser. When the purchaser has made full payment, the deed is transferred. This method can be used to purchase property with little or no money, but most sellers will require a credit check.

Investor Financing for Rental Property

Most banks will analyze the income-producing potential of a rental property rather than the equity you may have in the property. The lender is interested in knowing if the income produced by the property will cover expenses and pay the mortgage. Lenders look at the debt-repayment ratio (net operating income/total annual debt burden). Let's say you are considering buying and renovating a property that will produce $1,000 a month rent. That translates into $12,000 in rent, less a $1,000 allowance for one month's rent if the unit is unoccupied, and total expenses of $800. That comes out to a net operating income of $10,200.

Many lenders require at least a 1.2 debt-repayment ratio. A little bit of calculating shows that 10,200 divided by 1.2 gives you $8,500. This figure is the maximum debt load that this property can carry. Depending on the lender's specific requirements, most would lend you an amount that has an annual payment of less than $8,500. If the current rates are 7 percent for a 30-year fixed-rate loan, the lender will be willing to make a loan for up to $105,000.

The easiest way to calculate the size of the loan is to divide the debt load, $8,500, by 12 to get the monthly debt load of $708. Then go to the Internet and use one of the free mortgage calculators to find the size of the loan at 7 percent that produces a monthly payment of less than $708. It may take a couple of tries—if the payment comes out less than $708, then raise the loan amount; if more, lower the amount. You can also use the mortgage calculator in the Quicken computer software program, which will calculate the loan amount directly. Microsoft Money also has a mortgage calculator.

CHAPTER 7

FINDING AND EVALUATING PROPERTY

M ost investors remember the excitement and anxiety of searching for their first property. It can be a time-consuming process, with questions leading to more questions and feelings of uncertainty. You know you want to buy a house, you think you know where, but it all becomes fuzzy when you begin looking at listing sheets, reading For Sale by Owner advertisements, and walking through houses. Be patient and channel that uncertainty by probing for information. Just as in any start-up business or new job, you'll learn the process one step at a time.

Finding a "Good" House

The first concern in the fix-it-and-flip-it strategy is finding a "good" house—one that fits your budget, requires the appropriate amount of work for the time and money you plan to spend, and will command the resale price you desire.

Find Your Zone

Narrow your market by nailing down a neighborhood, and then learn everything you can about it. Choose an area that fits your budget and your marketing audience. Consider this target neighborhood as your work zone, and visit it frequently on foot, on bicycle, and by car. Walking or biking through an area gives you a close-to-home perspective where you can observe the people who live there, see the way they care for their homes, and take a good earthy look at housing up close and personal. Shop in the stores, eat in the local restaurants, frequent any local events, and get to know the neighborhood.

A drive through the neighborhood gives you a feel for traffic and a broader outlook of the area. To take the next step and look at property there, get connected with a good real estate agent to learn about current values and who lives there.

Your Agent, Your Ally

A typical way to meet an agent is to walk into his or her office, introduce yourself, and explain what you're looking for. Nothing coy about it, this direct approach lets you shake the agent's hand and see if he or she can help. Another way to meet an agent is through a friend's referral. And many investors meet an agent at an open house when he or she is the listing agent of the property.

A good real estate agent knows the neighborhood and will give you insights into the market, show you property, and ultimately shepherd you through the process of buying and taking possession of the house. When you look at property with an agent, he or she can tell you about comparable sales ("comps") for an idea of the current value of the property. If you are buying a house to rent it, the agent can tell you the rental history of a similar house and possibly find you a tenant.

A good agent makes it his or her business to know what's happening in a neighborhood that might affect the market—maybe it's a plan for a new road that will have an impact on a street or area, the expansion of the library, the closing of a school, or the crying need for rental property. Whatever is going on, a good agent has his or her finger on the pulse of the neighborhood. But like any salesperson, an agent emphasizes the positive and may not volunteer negative information. So ask a lot of questions.

As you work with an agent you'll find he or she can be a sounding board for ideas, not to mention a wealth of information about the nuances of real estate investing. Because a real estate agent deals with banks and lending companies on a regular basis, he or she can be a wealth of information about getting financing. The agent might be able to tell you which bank offers the lowest lending rate, which will lend to investors, and what percentage of a down payment they require.

At the selling end, a good agent knows the specifications that are required for a house to qualify for a federal or state mortgage-assistance program, so he or she can advise you of any special requirements like the amount of insulation that's needed. If you are targeting your property to sell to a first-time buyer, this information will guide you in selecting the materials to use when upgrading the property.

A good agent is used to a lot of questions, so ask them. Is a building permit needed for a new roof in the town, and if so, how much does it cost and where do you get one? Are there restrictions about owning a pet in a condominium unit? Is there a covenant against parking a truck in a neighborhood? Is there a time restriction in a vacation area for rental homes? You won't know the answers unless you ask.

Many contractors will tell you that some of their best customers are real estate agents who manage property and supervise repairs or maintenance on property they have listed. These agents know and hire tradespeople they can trust to clean carpeting, paint walls, fix plumbing leaks, and clean gutters. For a first-time investor, having a real estate agent with a Rolodex full of reliable contractors is a good beginning.

When a seller lists a property with a real estate company, the listing agent represents the seller. The agency receives on the average a 5 to 6 percent commission based on the selling price of the property. The commission is typically split between the listing agency and agent and the buyer's agent. Some agency or agents are "buyer brokers" who represent only the buyer and do not list property. There's more about services and arrangements between real estate agents in Chapter 10, "Buying the Property."

What You Bring to the Relationship

You'll get the most out of a relationship with a real estate agent by having a clear idea of what type of property you want to buy, whether you plan to resell or rent the property, where you want to buy, and how much you can spend. With that information an agent can fine-tune a search for property and help you focus on seeing listings that meet your criteria.

Not all agents are created equal. Some specialize (or want to) in high-end properties; some have little time for a budding investor. But a savvy agent knows a real estate investor is a good long-term client. By teaming up with an investor the agent gets a sale coming and going because investors use them on both sides of a transaction, first to find property and then to list it when it's ready for resale.

Finding Property and an Agent Online

Real estate sites on the Internet provide a useful overview of the housing market in particular areas with millions of house listings across the country. Just type the zip code in the search box and listings will appear, some with photos and virtual tours of the interior of the property. The sites offer links to finding property for sale and for rent, locating agents within that area, and maps that direct you to them. So as an overview the Internet gets high points on slicing and dicing listing information for the prospective buyer.

Unfortunately, what these sites don't do is update the information on a daily basis. You may see a property online and link to the listing agent to make an appointment to see the property, only to be told that the house is under contract. In a slow market when houses aren't selling quickly that's acceptable, but in a hot market, it's yesterday's news.

There's no substitute for a live person in a live real estate office with firsthand information about a property and the key to the front door to get you inside for a showing. To find an agent online, realtor.com, the site of the National Association of Realtors, is a good beginning point. All the real estate franchises have their own sites with similar "find a home" search engines and mapping based on the name of the town or its zip code. Some of these are remax.com, era.com, coldwellbanker.com, prudential.com, and longandfoster.com. Portals like MSN's House & Home and Yahoo!'s Real Estate have similar features.

Many investors are buying property in the country or in vacation areas with plans to improve the property and hold it for rental income before they retire there. The online real estate sites are a vehicle for screening a geographic region initially and comparing prices. For example, in an afternoon you can find the price difference between a two-bedroom, two-bath condo near the beach on the east and west coasts of Florida. You'll also find the rental costs and restrictions for different beach communities. The Internet is invaluable as a research tool to learn about an area and then make contact with an agent there.

If you know the address of a property and want to find out about the neighborhood, use a mapping service like mapquest.com. You enter a street address, city, and state, and the site renders a detailed map of its location. This can be a great way to prescreen property and discover if a house is in a good or less-than-desirable neighborhood like near railroad tracks, at the end of an airport runway, or in a commercial area. This information may help you rank prospective properties and spare you the time and effort of looking at properties you wouldn't consider.

LESSONS LEARNED

If you're planning to relocate to a new area and want to find an investment property, subscribe to the local newspaper or go to the paper's website to learn about local issues and read real estate ads. When you visit the area, stay at a bed and breakfast, where innkeepers are usually very amiable and willing to answer your questions about the area.

For Sale by Owner

Having a relationship with an agent does not prevent you from looking for property sold by owner. You can canvas a neighborhood for signs and follow the classifieds in local newspapers and magazines for advertisements of houses for sale by their owner.

The site forsalebyowner.com is a searchable database of properties in North America. They are partners with For Sale By Owner Publishing Network, which offers links to regional magazines with properties offered by owner.

Listing Sheets: Vital Signs of a House

If you've done your homework and have identified the housing market where you want to invest, you're ready to start evaluating property. The walk-through, or looking at houses, is a lot like prospecting, and we suggest doing some paperwork before the footwork. Remember, you're looking for a house with an opportunity to improve it through cosmetic changes, system upgrades, expansion potential, or any combination thereof. Use the property listing sheet as the first step before touring the house. Then create your own property profiles to analyze and compare all the properties you are considering as an investment.

There is a tremendous amount of property information on a real estate listing sheet, but at first glance it reads like a laundry list. But the more listing sheets you read and process, the more you begin to dissect the information and get an idea of what to expect when you tour the property. Before visiting a property, spend time reading between the lines of a listing sheet and use it as a starting point to raise questions.

Real estate agents use the Multiple Listing Service to electronically exchange listing information about properties. Years ago the information was kept on paper in binders or on note cards stored in shoe boxes and updated manually. While earlier information was cryptic and often contained limited descriptions, today agents can retrieve listing information in the blink of an eye and click of a mouse. This information is the vital signs of a house—approximate square footage, architectural style, year it was built, sizes and numbers of rooms, type of heating and cooling system, type of siding, condition of windows and roof, school district where it is located, which, if any, appliances are included, and of course, asking price and yearly taxes.

In the "Remarks" section of a listing sheet you'll find features the listing agent wants to highlight like, "Immaculate throughout this darling cottage." Depending on the writing skills of the listing agent, a listing sheet may exaggerate conditions with superlatives or provide no details at all.

In this listing sheet, Figure 7.1, note the Remarks section that cautions agents showing the property and prospective buyers by stating:

Figure 7.1

MLS#: TA3372159   **Metropolitan Regional Information Systems, Inc.**   Page: 1

			List Price: $34,000
MLS#: TA3372159	Status: SOLD	Own: Fee Simple, Sale	Old Map: 11K3
Contr Date: 07-JUN-2002	Set Date: 20-AUG-2002	Sold/Rented: $30,000	Subsidy: $0
DOMM/DOMP: 540 /592			
Adv Sub: ST. MICHAELS		HOA: $0.00 C/C:	TBM Map: 107
Style: Bungalow	Type: Detached	Total Taxes: $379	Area: 1-2
Year Built: 1935	Model:	LS-SF/Acre: 10000/ 0.23	Total Fin SF: 0
BR: 2 FB: 1 HB:	Const: Wood		#Lvls: 0 #Fpls: 0
Basement: NO		Park: On-site Prk/Rent	
H Fuel/C Fuel: Oil / None		Wtr/Swr: Public / Public Sewer	
Water Front/View/Access: N/N/N		Dock Conveys: N	Vacation: NO

List/Upd: 14-DEC-2000/27-DEC-2002 Listing Co: RE/MAX BLAKENEY, LLC
Remarks: Handyman special on large lot in town.

"Handyman special." That's a phrase like "needs a face-lift" and "fixer-upper" that often describes a property ripe for rehabbing.

Red Flags to Look for at the First Showing

The listing sheet is your first exposure to a property, but it's basically a fact sheet used as a sales tool. You won't find negative information on the sheet, so it's up to you to see the property and do some tire kicking.

Your first impression of a property is important, and your reaction will probably be similar to that of other prospective buyers. Your mission is to look beyond its present condition and visualize the property after you have improved it. But don't overlook aspects of the property that can't be changed economically and still yield a profit. Here are some trouble spots to be aware of:

Standing Water on the Lot

Standing water on the property can be a sign of poor drainage, which can be the cause of a wet basement or a settling or cracked foundation. Be sure to walk around the lot and note any damp, mossy areas and places where the grass does not grow. Some drainage problems are easy to fix, but if the lot seems damp or you see standing water, take note to investigate further.

Water and Moisture Damage

Rain, snow, and moisture can cause damage to several parts of a house, such as wood rotting in the soffits where there's no ventilation, or moss growing on roof shingles or the siding on the north side of the house. These telltale signs are a tip-off to look for other indications of water damage throughout the house, such as roof rafters for signs of rotten sheeting or rafters.

Dampness can also promote the growth of mold and mildew, which mean more trouble. Water damage can be prevented with proper maintenance, but if neglected over time, the damage can be expensive to repair. Any signs of neglect should cause you to take a second look.

Structural Problems

Major structural problems such as a cracked or settling foundation can be very expensive to fix. Unless you can get a firm estimate on the repair cost and use the amount to negotiate a lower purchase price, don't consider the property. Carefully explore the cause of large cracks in walls, especially in corners. Large horizontal cracks can be a tip-off to foundation movement, which is not a good thing.

Underground Tanks

Underground tanks of any type can become an environmental disaster if they have been leaking for years. Be sure to check the location of heating oil, propane, or gasoline tanks on the property. You do not want to discover when excavating the foundation for an addition that you have a large oil spill in the backyard.

Well and Septic Systems

If the property does not have public water and sewer, ask about the condition of its well and septic system. Septic field failure can produce wet areas and poor drainage, which can indicate a problem.

How Long Will It Last?

Appliances have a useful life, but after that it becomes more expensive to repair than replace the unit. Carefully note the condition of each appliance. Even if you plan a kitchen makeover, many times you can reuse the appliances. Refer to Table 7.1 to learn how long appliances last.

Inspecting 101: Make a Property Profile

A property profile is a detailed checklist to help you inspect and evaluate the potential of every house you look at. Use it as you walk through

Table 7.1 Average Useful Life of Major Home Appliances

Appliance	Average Useful Life*
Air conditioner, room	2 years
Cooktop, double, built-in	21 years
Cooktop, single, built-in	13 years
Dehumidifier	11 years
Dishwasher	13 years
Disposal	12 years
Dryer	13 years
Oven, built-in	16 years
Range, double-oven	18 years
Range, drop-in, single-oven	11 years
Range, slide-in, single-oven	17 years
Refrigerator	14 years
Trash compactor	4 years
Washer, front-load	11 years
Washer, top-load	14 years

Source: National Family Opinion, Inc. (NFO), 1996 survey

*The age of an appliance when it must be replaced because it cannot be repaired or costs too much to repair

a house to help form an educated evaluation. It takes some imagination and experience to see through a neglected house that's dirty and distressed. The profile should help you see the Cinderella in a less-than-perfect house and focus on its potential.

As you walk through a house, look at the layout and floor plan. Is there an unfinished attic suitable for expansion? What's the condition of the walls, cabinets, floors, and appliances? What about the heating and cooling systems? The items on the checklist remind you to inspect all the elements of the house so you can make an informed buying decision.

Use property profiles to weigh the pros and cons of several properties by making one for every house under consideration. As the number of houses you walk through increases, they tend to blur together and it's difficult to recall the distinctions among them. Spread the profiles out on a table and use the information about each house to either eliminate it from consideration or raise it to the top of the pile. While these property profiles keep you straight and help you remember distinct features and trouble spots, they also provide a handy way to make notes and observations.

Use a clipboard or notebook for the property profile sheet along with paper to make a sketch of the floor plan. Bring a pen, measuring tape, and pair of binoculars (to look at the roof and chimney) when you walk through the property. If permitted, bring a camera so you'll have photographs or digital images of the house.

Using the Profile to Compare Properties

We all make different kinds of lists; some are short and cryptic, and others verge on being anal-retentive. Err on the side of being anal when you're touring a property as a potential investment because the more you record on the profile, the more information you gather that will help you make the most enlightened decision to invest.

Some information is on the listing sheet of the property, but it's wise to verify that it's accurate. As a matter of fact, on the bottom of every listing sheet there is a disclaimer about accuracy. So it's in your best interest to confirm that the type and number of kitchen appliances is correct, that a washer and dryer is included, and that the third bedroom, although small, does indeed have a closet. You'll develop your own code for using the checklist. Circle the "red flags" or signs of neglect and concern when you see a rusty air conditioner or missing roof shingles. Better yet, take copious notes and comment on the condition with a short notation.

Make the checklist work for you and your style of observation. Figure 7.2 is an example of notations from a property profile.

Copy or scan these property profile sheets (Figure 7.3), and customize them to the types of houses in your area. For example, if the houses have no basements, delete that category. Add items that are appropriate for the type of property you're considering for investment.

Figure 7.2 Sample Property Profile Notes

INSPECTION ITEMS	NOTES
Living, Dining, Family Room	
Walls and ceilings	*ugly wallpaper, gotta go*
Built-ins or fireplace	*nice mantel*
Bathroom	
Tub/shower	*mildew in corners*
Toilet	*flushes slow*
Lawn and Garden	
Back and side yard	*large tree stump to remove; nice garden beds, need weeding*

Figure 7.3 Property Profile

Address:

Date of inspection:

Agent:

INSPECTION ITEMS   **NOTES**

Exterior Entrance

Walkways, driveway and stairs
  leading to the house   _____

Lawn, plantings, and trees in
  front yard   _____

Front door   _____

Living, dining, family room

Walls and ceilings   _____

Doors and windows   _____

Flooring   _____

Number of electrical outlets   _____

Lighting fixtures   _____

Built-ins or fireplace   _____

Closet   _____

Other features   _____

Bathroom

Walls and ceiling   _____

Flooring   _____

Lighting fixtures   _____

Doors and windows   _____

Number of GFCI electrical outlets   _____

INSPECTION ITEMS	NOTES
Cabinets	_____
Countertops	_____
Ventilation	_____
Tub/shower	_____
Toilet	_____
Sink and faucet	_____
Closet	_____
Other features	_____

Kitchen

Walls and ceilings	_____
Lighting fixtures	_____
Doors and windows	_____
Flooring	_____
Number of GFCI electrical outlets	_____
Cabinets/islands	_____
Countertops	_____
Ventilation	_____
Appliances and their power sources	_____
range	_____
refrigerator	_____
dishwasher	_____
disposal	_____
Sink and faucet	_____
Other features	_____

INSPECTION ITEMS	NOTES

Attic

Unfinished—usable as storage
or living space _____

    thickness of insulation _____

    height at peak _____

    location of stairs _____

    electrical and lighting _____

Basement

Walls and framing _____

    Signs of termite or pest damage _____

Unfinished—usable as storage
or living space _____

    high water mark sign on walls _____

    height of lowest pipe or duct _____

    location of stairs _____

    location of exterior access _____

    proximity to furnace _____

Finished _____

    walls and ceilings _____

    doors and windows _____

    flooring _____

    number of electrical outlets _____

    lighting fixtures _____

    closet or storage _____

    other features _____

Sump pump _____

Ventilation _____

INSPECTION ITEMS	NOTES

Laundry

Wash tub _____

Number of GFCI electrical outlets _____

Power source for washer/dryer _____

Washer/dryer units _____

Systems and Mechanics

Electrical panel _____

    location _____

    amperage and voltage rating _____

    number of circuits _____

    limited or expandable _____

Heating system _____

Air conditioning system or
    window units _____

Hot water heater _____

Water-softening system _____

Exterior of house

Doors and windows _____

Storm doors and windows _____

Siding _____

Roof _____

    missing or curling shingles _____

Chimney _____

    loose bricks or flashing _____

Porches _____

    screens _____

    potential to enclose _____

INSPECTION ITEMS	NOTES
Drainage and gutters	_____
tight fitting gutters and downspouts	_____
pooling water around foundation	_____
Foundation and crawl space	_____
signs of termite or pest damage	_____
wet or dry	_____
insulation	_____
ventilation	_____

Garage and Outbuildings

Foundation and soundness of structure	_____
Condition of siding, doors, windows	_____
Signs of termite or pest damage	_____

Lawn and Garden

Fencing	_____
location of posts (who owns it?)	_____
condition	_____
does it mark property line?	_____
Back and side yard	_____
grass and/or weeds	_____
overgrown shrubbery	_____
diseased trees	_____
overhanging tree limbs	_____

CHAPTER 8

HOME IMPROVEMENT FROM AN INVESTOR'S PERSPECTIVE

The housing stock of the United States is old. Sixty-one million houses are more than 25 years old, and 24 million are between 16 and 25 years old. Most of these older houses were built to a different set of buyer expectations. Changes in family life and new technologies and building materials have made upgrading the aging housing stock big business. That's a lot of houses for real estate investors to improve and upgrade.

The underlying principle of *Fix It and Flip It* is that with careful planning you can purchase property below market value, make improvements to it that increase its value well above the cost of the improvements, and then sell it for a profit. Any house that you may consider a candidate for investment does not exist in a vacuum. A particular property located in one neighborhood may represent a real opportunity, but that same property in a different location may not be such a hot prospect. There are several factors that determine the value of real estate, and each of these factors must be considered when sizing up a potential property.

Factors Influencing the Value of Property

Besides "buy low, sell high" the next most quoted real estate cliché is "location, location, location." Location is important, but it's not the only factor that determines the value of a property. One of the challenges you face when looking at investment property is not only to assess the current value of the property but also to assess its potential value.

You want to buy property that is below its current market potential. The property is worth exactly what a buyer is prepared to pay for it—no more and no less. You are the buyer, so you set the value of the property when you purchase it. The question you have to answer—and this determines your profit potential—is, Can the property be changed in some way to attract another buyer to pay more for the property than the last buyer? That's you.

Let's take a look at all of the factors that influence the value of a property.

Location and Market

When talking about location it's helpful to think of those animated shots you see on TV starting with a picture of the world and then continually zooming in until it's a scene of a particular part of a city or town. Taken from that perspective, location can have several nuances.

National Market

The national economy in general has an effect on real estate. National events like terrorism, war, or an economic recession affect real estate markets. A rise in interest rates from the historically low levels we have experienced at the turn of the millennium will raise the cost of home ownership. But over the long haul, real estate has been a great investment for many people.

However, changes in the national economy can affect a short-term fix-it-and-flip-it strategy. As you search for properties and plan the renovations, don't operate in a vacuum; keep an eye on the national economy. If you purchase property at the start of a downturn in the economy, it makes it harder, but not impossible, to sell for a profit during the slump. If this is the case, you can alter your strategy from fix it and flip it to fix to occupy or fix to rent.

Regional Market

Inside the United States there are different regions of the country that at any given time experience unique real estate markets. Depending on where you are located, your regional market may be different from other regions of the country. What is happening in California is not necessarily happening in the Midwest.

Be aware of your regional real estate market. To purchase property at a bargain price in a hot market may not be such a bargain if the market cools down. For example, in the mid-1980s we relocated from the Midwest to the East Coast. The particular area we settled in was experiencing a red-hot market. In fact, our purchase offers were passed over for full-price offers with no mortgage contingency. Less than a year later the market cooled off, and it took until the mid-1990s for the market to gain that much steam again. If you purchased property at the peak of that overheated market you experienced little or no appreciation during the time the market was flat.

It's difficult if not impossible to time the real estate market, which usually doesn't swing as fast as the equity markets, so it's important to keep regional economic conditions on your radar screen to realize the full potential of your investment.

Local Market

The camera zooming in to the individual houses of a neighborhood is exactly how most people in the real estate market look for a house. The location of a potential investment in a neighborhood is a key factor determining its value. There always will be the good and bad sides of the tracks. Entire neighborhoods can change and be revitalized, but it doesn't happen overnight. Purchasing fix-up property in a transitional neighborhood before it is clear the neighborhood is on an upswing is speculation, and many investors have made tremendous profits doing it. But others like us are willing to buy property in a premium neighborhood because we know that when it is improved it will command a premium price. Good schools, low crime, good transportation, and economic growth greatly influence the value of property.

Comparing Properties

Most professional real estate agents that you establish a relationship with will do what is called a comparative market analysis at no charge. The analysis is an examination of house sale records in recent weeks or months to determine what houses in a given price range, size, location, and general condition have been listed at and what the actual selling price was. When you are looking at these comps, don't forget to factor in the neighborhood.

To understand what buyers expect in a house at the price you want to sell your investment property for, look at the characteristics of similar property that has recently sold. For example, if you buy a house for $100,000 and hope to resell it for $150,000, you will have to change the property to meet the expectations of buyers shopping for $150,000 houses. The difference in characteristics of $100,000 houses from the $150,000 houses tells you about the size, features, and condition of the higher-valued property.

Most real estate companies have their own website, which has handy search tools that allow you to screen properties on a wide variety of criteria. Filter your search to display property with sales prices close to $150,000. You may have to visit several sites to make a comprehensive list. The difference here is that you will have access only to the asking prices, not what the properties actually sold for.

Get the Facts

The decision to purchase is made on the individual property, but the decision is not made in a vacuum. Several factors—location, size of the property, its features and condition, how it compares with similar property, and how many similar properties are available—are taken together to determine the value of the property.

Location

The location of a property is one of the most important factors in determining its value. You must compare properties that are in the same location. All other factors being the same, similar properties located in different areas can have vastly different values. Differences in location, even in the same general area, will affect value. For example, a property located at the edge of what is considered a good neighborhood may be several thousand dollars less expensive than a property located squarely in the neighborhood.

There is also the possibility that the lower-valued location will become highly valued. The more unlikely that this will happen, the bigger the difference in price. Investing in up-and-coming locations can be very rewarding, but we have left this to the more aggressive. Just remember that when comparing investments, their locations must be considered comparable.

Size
A major factor in evaluating property is its size. All other factors being equal, the larger the property the more valuable it tends to be. The size of the lot and the number of bedrooms and bathrooms all must be considered when comparing several potential properties.

Condition
The condition of the house is the variable that will probably be hardest to compare. Since you are looking at property that needs TLC, it will be in less than perfect condition. This is difficult if not impossible to do before you actually visit the property. So for the initial screening, there is not much you can compare until you actually make an inspection. So go back and go over Chapter 7. Make your lists and then compare.

Features
Garages, porches, fireplaces, and other features like these add to the property's value. Carefully list all the features of each property so you can ferret out the property with the best overall value.

Once you have the data you can compare the properties that have recently sold or are valued around the target sales price for the property you are analyzing. How are the properties different? The same? What do the higher-valued or -priced properties have that the property you may purchase lacks? The answer to these questions will give you direction on the best improvements to make to meet the buyer's expectations.

Meeting Buyers' Expectations

Whatever repairs, upgrades, or improvements you do to a house, be sure they meet the local building code requirements. Any violations or repairs not fixed that come up while selling a house can easily give the buyer second thoughts about the property, not to mention a legal reason to back out of the contract. That said, make repairs and improvements that matter based on comparable houses in the neighborhood.

Make Repairs

We look at repairs as a kid looks at doing homework. You have to do it to get a passing grade. Teachers expect it as a minimum, and they really like it when you do extra-credit work. A home buyer who is paying market value expects a house will be in good repair and hires a home inspector to look for deficiencies and report them.

If you're considering buying a house and one of the improvements needed is a new roof that will cost $10,000 (possibly much more if the roof sheeting requires replacement), look at your research about comparable houses. If you find they sell for $115,000, there's no reason to buy the house. You'll spend way too much money on the roof alone. In our experience, as long as the roof looks OK and passes an inspection, buyers are satisfied. Given the choice among two or more comparable houses, most buyers are unwilling to pay the full premium for a house with a new roof. No doubt the new roof will make the house easier to sell, but few buyers choose to pay the full $10,000 extra.

Don't Mess with the Structure

Another fact we discovered is that costs can easily get out of hand as soon as you start to modify the structure or systems of the house. The easiest fix-ups and the most profitable are those that don't require major structural changes like moving kitchen and bathroom fixtures, or opening up load-bearing walls and adding rooms outside the original footprint of the building. We have better success building second-floor dormers or decks or moving non-load-bearing walls. We discuss these in Chapter 13, "Space-Expanding Possibilities."

Certainly it's possible to make major structural changes to a property and increase its value far beyond the cost of the upgrade, but we'd consider it only if we were going to live in the property over a period of years so we'd have inflation working for us too.

Kitchens and Bathrooms

Improvements to kitchens and bathrooms will cost and pay back the most. And they're the two key rooms that buyers look at very seriously. Even buyers on a shoestring budget want the best possible kitchen and bathrooms they can get. We've never bought a house on which we didn't do a lot of work in both of these rooms because—let's face it—they are the most used rooms in a house. In Chapter 11 you'll find quick fixes and face-lifts that we think get the best bang for the buck.

The upgrades in a kitchen can range from a basic cosmetic face-lift of paint, flooring, and appliances to expanding the kitchen into an adjoining room and replacing everything from the ceiling to the floor and all the cabinets and appliances.

Even buyers of a two-bedroom home expect at least a full bath and a half bath to solve the crunch when everyone is getting ready for work and school in the morning. So by making a one-bath house into a two-bath house by using existing space, you'll recoup the investment. In a bathroom the upgrade can be as basic as scrubbing and wallpapering to gutting it and rebuilding everything with a new bathtub and shower, vanity and countertop, tile, and lighting. In some cases it involves changing the arrangement of fixtures to make a small space work harder.

In Chapter 14 there's information about using the design services offered at home centers to redesign a kitchen or bathroom.

The *Remodeling 2002 Cost vs. Value Report* compares the estimated cost of a professionally installed renovation with the value it is likely to add to the home a year later. The report indicates that home owners who invest in a midrange kitchen remodel estimated at $43,213 will recover 67 percent and an upscale kitchen remodel at $70,368 comes in at 80 percent. A bathroom remodel costing $9,720 recoups 88 percent of that cost. The addition of a bathroom for $15,058 that is built within the existing footprint of the home comes in at 94 percent (source: Remodeling Online).

If you're living in the house while making improvements and the neighborhood supports a luxury bathroom or a gourmet kitchen, you may be able to rationalize their expense. But do the research and find out if comparable properties feature high-end upgrades and what they're selling for before you jump in.

Avoid the Extreme

Specialized areas like wine cellars, dedicated gyms, tennis courts, and swimming pools seldom give a good return on the investment—that is, unless they are the norm in the neighborhood. Still, the expense is seldom recoverable.

DOING THE MATH

In the preceding chapters we have gone over the strategy we use to evaluate a property for its potential as a fix-it-and-flip-it candidate. In this chapter we do the numbers. However you look at the business of real estate investing, unless you are in the rental business, the profit has to come from the difference between the purchase price and the sale price. The difference must be large enough to cover all costs.

This is a simple formula: (sales price) − (purchase price + cost) = profit. If you look carefully at the three variables in this equation you realize that each is made up of many smaller variables. Some you have direct control over, like the purchase price and cost; others, like the sales price, you have to estimate. Here's a look at the three variables and how they relate to different purchase scenarios.

Purchase Price

The most important variable in the equation is the purchase price. Much of your potential profit in any real estate project is determined the moment you settle on a purchase price. If you overpay for the property, the added value of your improvements can't be fully realized.

The real challenge is that most property with any potential will eventually find a buyer. If a buyer who plans to live in the property overpays, he or she has time for the property to appreciate. Improvements made during the occupation are made not necessarily to generate a profit but to improve the livability and the home owner's enjoyment of living there. Eventually the buyer may get money out of the deal.

You, the investor, on the other hand, must purchase the property at a low enough price to afford the necessary improvements needed for the property to reach its full market value. If you plan to upgrade the property you still must have a low enough purchase price so it supports the planned improvements. With this in mind you must establish a purchase price we call the "target purchase price" for the property that assures you don't overpay.

The target purchase price that you can afford to pay for a particular property may be far from what the seller has in mind. Remember that we defined the value of any property as what a buyer will pay, not what the seller is asking.

Costs

The next variables in the profit equation are the costs of purchasing and holding the property, costs of all planned repairs and improvements, sales costs, and, of course, a profit. Some of the costs are easier to calculate than others. Here is a rundown of the major costs involved in fixing up a property for resale.

Closing Costs

At the closing of a real estate deal certain costs of the transaction are apportioned to the buyer and seller. The buyer pays for an appraisal, survey, property transfer taxes, and legal fees. If the real estate taxes are paid, then a rebate is given the seller; if not, the seller pays for his or her share of the tax bill. Of course, you also have to settle up with the bank and pay any fees they require to execute the loan.

These are but a few of the possible closing costs (see Chapter 10, "Buying the Property," for more details), and they can add up to thousands of dollars. Most of the fees and taxes are set fees or a percentage of the sale price. It is possible to make an accurate estimate of what these costs will be. This may seem like a big project at first, but the type of

deals you will be doing are the same, so after the first exercise, estimating the closing costs for your next project will be easy. A real estate
broker or the bank that is financing the deal can give you a sample closing statement.

Holding Costs

The holding costs include interest on the loan, taxes, and utilities. The
length of time you plan to hold the property affects these costs. Unless
the project can be turned around in a month or so and put back on the
market, use a year as the standard holding time. A fix-it project that
takes three or four months to complete may require several more
months to sell.

We found it a great motivator to keep the job on schedule if we broke
the holding cost down to a monthly figure. Knowing that a project costs
$1,800 per month just to own the property is a great motivator to get the
job done. Time is money, and if you take this a bit further you find that
in this case every hour you haven't sold the property costs you $2.50.

Repairs and Improvements

These can run the gamut from a simple paint and polish to a second-
floor expansion. It is essential that you have a good idea what these costs
will be. The challenge is that you don't have a lot of time to pull these
costs together. If the property has potential, other buyers will be looking at it and may be able to act more quickly than you can.

It is not too difficult to figure repair costs. In Chapter 12, "Estimating Fix-Up Costs," we give you some ballpark figures for typical repairs
and small projects. Use these as a baseline to develop your own set of
costs. In addition, both R. S. Means and Craftsman Books produce
yearly construction cost books that are helpful in putting together a
quick estimate. The books have general square-foot costs for major
remodeling and repair work and provide material and labor data that
can be adjusted regionally.

All real estate purchase agreements have an inspection clause that
allows for a home inspection when you can get more accurate estimates
for the costs of improvements. On the inspection day, go through the

house with the inspector and ask for a realistic cost for work required. If unexpected problems are found, you can work with the seller to resolve the issues, or you can decide to back out of the purchase agreement.

The repairs and improvements cost represents a major portion of the project's overall expense. If after you calculate the total cost you arrive at an unrealistically low purchase price, some adjustments are in order. In some cases the market will not support the cost of the repairs and improvements and return a decent profit; if that's the case, it's better to find out before you purchase the property.

Contingency

Like any other business, fixing up property for resale has its risks. This is what the contingency fund is all about. While changing a kitchen faucet seems straightforward, it can get grim if you break a rusted pipe in the wall. Something that was budgeted for $100 suddenly costs $400. The contingency is an important part of the budget because it allows you to anticipate the unexpected and provide sufficient funds if they are needed. Because you include the contingency amount as an expense up front to lower the purchase price, not having the expense of a broken pipe ends up on the bottom line. The older and more run-down the property, the higher the contingency fund should be.

Sales Costs

Every real estate transaction has costs to both the seller and purchaser. We estimate these costs separately from the sales costs because the value of the property is different. The largest component of the selling costs is the commission paid to the real estate broker, which a steady customer can negotiate. Both seller and buyer get the same closing statement, so you can estimate the selling costs.

Profit

This line is considered an expense because the difference between the purchase price and selling price must contain the profit. The figure is the actual cash that you hope to realize after the dust settles, the property is sold, and all loans and bills are paid. Because most of the money to buy and improve the property comes from the lender, even a small amount of cash can represent a hefty return on your investment, namely the down payment.

Sales Price

It would be nice if you could add up all the costs, decide on a profit, and then add the figures to the price paid for the property and place it back on the market. You can if you buy the property right. That is what the Property Analysis worksheet will help you calculate.

Any of the real estate websites on the Internet are a good place to take an initial look for comparable properties. The search results will give you a ballpark idea of the value of the house or at least the going asking prices. As we suggested earlier, your real estate broker can also prepare a market analysis of comparable houses that have recently sold. If you have expanded and improved a property, look for comparable properties in the same neighborhood and condition.

Time

One important variable that is not explicitly stated is time. Owning real estate has costs: interest on the loan, taxes, utilities, items like that. The longer you own the property the more costs you incur. But over that same period most real estate appreciates, and this has historically offset the costs. Unless the local real estate market is very hot, appreciation over a short time won't cover the holding costs. But open that horizon to several years or more, and the property can appreciate enough to cover these costs. That is the most appealing characteristic of a real estate investment.

With some exceptions, a fix-up-and-sell property with a short window of ownership that appreciates adds little to the bottom line. A fix-up-to-occupy project with a window of ownership of several years may experience considerable appreciation during the time of renovation and occupancy.

Analysis of a Fix-It-and-Flip-It Property

When considering a property that has fix-up but not expansion possibilities, we would do the research to find out its value when upgraded. Then, working backward from the estimated price, we subtract all costs and profit. This number is the most we'd pay and expect to make the repairs and sell the property for a profit. This is, of course, not set in stone, but unless we modified the plan, it's the most we'd pay.

The purchase analysis side of the worksheet in Figure 9.1 shows an analysis of a two-bedroom home in poor condition. Let's say after completing a market analysis of comparable property we decided that the house would be worth $168,000 with repairs and improvements completed. We'd enter that figure in the Estimated Improved Value row, and then we'd subtract estimated costs (for closing, holding, and repairs) of $15,500. We'd anticipate and subtract a $2,000 contingency and a $7,000 profit as well as estimated sales costs of $15,000. The result would be our target purchase price ($128,500). After putting 10 percent down, the standard mortgage would be for $115,650.

Remember that this is a worksheet and there are variables here that can be fine-tuned. If after working with the numbers the target purchase price turned out so low that it would be an insult to the seller, we'd probably pass on the property or make a lowball offer with the data to back up our reasoning. Because the bank would require an appraisal, we would have the appraiser make two reports: one that states the value of the property as-is to support the mortgage, the other with the value of the property after the fix-up.

Then we'd get a short-term loan, second mortgage, or construction loan—however the bank wanted to structure the deal for the estimated improvement cost. The only money we'd have in the project would be the down payment of $12,850. If everything went as planned, we'd expect to make a good return on our investment. (We arrive at 54 percent by dividing the expected profit of $7,000 by the down payment of $12,850.) The project would be figured on a one-year holding time; if we finished sooner, the holding costs and interest would be less and we'd get a larger profit.

The right side of the worksheet is an example of an actual sale of the property. It might go like this: the repairs went over budget by $1,000,

Figure 9.1 Sample Property Analysis Worksheet:
Fix-It-and-Flip-It Property

Closing Costs	$1,500	
Holding Costs	$7,000	
Repairs	$7,000	
Total Expenses		$15,500
Contingency	$2,000	
Profit	$7,000	
Total Contingency/Profit		$9,000
Estimated Sales Costs		$15,000
Target Purchase Price		**$128,500**
10 Percent Down		$12,850
First Mortgage		$115,650
Construction Loan		$15,500
Estimated Return on Investment (Before Tax)	**54 percent**	
Real Estate Commission	$9,720	
Overbudget Expenses	$1,000	
Total Costs		$11,320
Net		$150,680
Repay First Mortgage	$115,650	
Repay Construction Loan	$15,500	
Total Paydown		$131,150
Cash Out		**$19,530**
Investment		$13,850
Profit		**$5,680**
Return on Investment (Before Tax)	**41 percent**	

and the best offer for the property was $162,000. The cash flow went to pay off the sales, closing costs, and overbudget expenses (a total of $11,320).

The net cash from the sale was $150,680, and from that amount the loans were paid off, leaving $19,530. (Remember that the bank loaned the money for the repairs.) The down payment of $12,850 and the $1,000 overbudget expenses were returned, leaving a profit of $5,680, a nice 41 percent return.

Analysis of an Expand-and-Flip-It Property

The same worksheet can be used to analyze a property that will be expanded, but the initial approach would be a bit different. Instead of making a market analysis for the property as it is, you'd make a market analysis of properties that compare to how it will be after the modifications. For example, this analysis is for a two-bedroom, one-bath house that could be expanded into a four-bedroom, two-bath house (Figure 9.2).

We determined that the modified house could be sold for at least $225,000. The worksheet would be used exactly in the same way as it was with the fix-it-and-flip-it property to calculate a target purchase price. After accounting for all expenses, the worksheet helps us determine that we should not offer more than $149,000 for the property if we expect to meet the profit goal. You see that the estimated costs for repairs and remodeling are much higher than for a repair-only property.

Copy the Property Analysis Worksheet in Figure 9.3 and use it for your analysis.

Figure 9.2 Sample Property Analysis Worksheet: Expand-and-Flip-It Property

Purchase Analysis

Estimated Improved Value		$225,000
Less:		
Closing Costs	$3,000	
Holding Costs	$13,000	
Repairs	$5,000	
Improvements	$25,000	
Total Expenses		$46,000
Contingency	$5,000	
Profit	$10,000	
Total Contingency/Profit		$15,000
Estimated Sales Costs	$15,000	$15,000
Target Purchase Price		**$149,000**
10 Percent Down		$14,900
First Mortgage		$134,100
Construction Loan		$46,000

**Estimated Return on Investment
  (Before Tax)**   **67 percent**

Actual Sale

Sale Price		$223,000
Closing Costs	$3,000	
Real Estate Commission	$13,380	
Overbudget Expenses	$1,000	
Total		$17,380
Net		$205,620
Repay First Mortgage	$134,100	
Repay Construction Loan	$46,000	
Total Paydown		$180,100
Cash Out		**$25,520**
Investment		$15,900
Profit		**$9,620**

**Return on Investment
  (Before Tax)**   **61 percent**

Figure 9.3 Property Analysis Worksheet

Purchase Analysis

Estimated Improved Value _____

Less: _____

  Closing Costs _____

  Holding Costs _____

  Repairs _____

  Improvements _____

Total Expenses _____

  Contingency _____

  Profit _____

Total Contingency/Profit _____

Estimated Sales Costs _____

Target Purchase Price _____

10 Percent Down _____

First Mortgage _____

Construction Loan _____

**Estimated Return on Investment
(Before Tax)** _____

Actual Sale _____

Sales Price _____

Closing Costs _____

Real Estate Commission _____

Overbudget Expenses _____

Total _____

Net _____

Repay First Mortgage _____

Repay Construction Loan _____

Total Paydown _____

Cash Out _____

Investment _____

Profit _____

**Return on Investment
(Before Tax)** _____

CHAPTER 10

BUYING THE PROPERTY

Savvy investors agree that you make your profit when you *buy* property, not when you sell it. If you don't buy it right, meaning below the market value, there's little chance of making a profit. Before you make an offer on a property it's good to know how that money is divvied up.

The main way a broker makes his or her money is by listing property (it's a broker's bread and butter) and receiving a commission or percentage of the sales price when it is sold. Another is selling other brokers' listings and receiving a commission. When a broker sells property he or she listed, that broker takes the lion's share. The office of the listing agent also gets a percentage, which covers their cost of doing business, advertising, and so on. So at a property closing many checks are cut dividing up the agreed-on selling price of the property. The amount of commission paid to brokers varies depending on the state where they are licensed; in general, it is 3 to 7 percent of the selling price.

Investing in real estate introduces you to a cast of financial and housing professionals—bankers, loan officers, appraisers, home inspectors, and insurance agents—and all of them will require your attention. They present you with requests for information and forms to fill out for processing either in person or online. The scene is orchestrated by your real estate broker, who keeps things on track and assures that all the paperwork and processing are completed so the closing happens on time and with all the parties happy.

So, you've screened several properties, run the numbers on all of them, and found a house that's below the market value and ripe for rehabbing. You have done your homework about getting a mortgage, you have all your financing lined up, and you're ready to make an offer. Here's what to expect.

Doing the Deal

First, you make an offer to purchase the property. Listen to the advice of your broker, but remember your target purchase price; don't be afraid to make a low offer. If the property is new on the market, you might not have much leverage, but if it's been for sale for a month and no one's made an offer, perhaps the market has softened. The seller can make a counteroffer (asking you to up the ante and pay more), and you can meet the higher price by accepting it or countering with another offer.

The volleying between offers and counteroffers is where the negotiating skills of the brokers comes into play and where they earn their money. The selling price as well as the terms of the contract can also be things to negotiate. For example, if you make an $89,900 offer for a property and want to close the deal and take possession in two months, it might trump an offer for $93,000 if the other buyer's closing date is four months away. Finalizing the sale, getting the money, and moving may be worth more to the seller than a larger amount. You and the seller may agree to a lower price of the property based on the estimated cost of the repairs or replacements specified in the inspection report, which can be to your advantage.

You may offer cash as an incentive to the seller so waiting for financing and approval isn't necessary. A cash offer translates to a fast sale, which can be very enticing to a seller who is leaving the area and wants to move quickly.

Yes, you should have some wiggle room in negotiating the price with the seller, but don't stray from your target purchase price for the property. Know your limit and stick to it, and don't let emotions get in the way. Just remember that there will always be another house that's ripe for rehabbing.

Leave Yourself an Out

Make sure any contract you sign has two contingency clauses. One clause should let you out of the deal if the property doesn't pass an inspection and you and the seller can't agree on how to resolve the problem. Unless you make a cash offer, a mortgage contingency is also necessary. This clause states that the purchase is contingent on you obtaining a reasonable mortgage in a stipulated period of time.

The contract states that a down payment or earnest money is deposited in an account and that money is applied to the sales price if the deal goes through but is returned to you if the deal falls apart.

If you haven't already been approved for a mortgage to cover the cost of the property, that's the next step. This is covered in Chapter 6, "Finding the Money." Your next step is hiring a home inspector to examine the physical condition of the house and property and make a written report of its condition, including any defects and possible future problems. When the inspection is completed and the property is reported to be sound by the inspector, you've bought yourself a house.

Hiring a Home Inspector

There are two trade groups representing home inspectors, and a visit to their websites is a good idea to familiarize yourself with the guidelines for a proper inspection and to know what to expect from one. At ashi.com you'll find information about the American Society of Home Inspectors; nahi.org is the site for the National Association of Home Inspectors. Membership in these groups means the inspector has an expertise in home construction and agrees to a certain standard of conduct. For between $300 and $500, an inspector will make a thorough examination of the property and give you an itemized report of what he or she found.

Use the sites to locate a home inspector in your area or get a reference for an inspector from someone who has bought a home in the area. Many banks, lenders, and real estate brokers suggest inspectors they work with on a regular basis.

When you call to schedule an inspection, ask if the inspector carries insurance to cover any mistakes he or she makes and if some or all of the structural and mechanical systems of the house are examined.

Schedule the inspection so you can attend, and ask questions as you go through the house.

Going to Settlement: Closing the Deal

Do you need a lawyer to represent you when you are buying a house? Maybe yes, maybe no. But if the purchase is your first home, it's a good idea to hire one to represent your interests and thoroughly explain the process before it happens. If any problems arise, a lawyer can expedite the issue and move the deal to closure. Don't choose just any lawyer; select one that specializes in property closings. You don't need a trial lawyer who is good in the courtroom; you want someone versed in property settlements in the area where the house is located. Many law offices field this work to paralegals who go through the process regularly. Ask friends or your broker for references, and talk to them about what the lawyer charges and what services he or she provides.

Closing Costs for a Buyer

After you have applied for a mortgage, the lending institution is required to send you a good-faith estimate of your closing costs and confirm the percentage rate of the loan. These closing costs associated with buying a house cover a laundry list of taxes, insurance, reports, searches, and charges for document preparation, tax service, notary service, and state recording fees.

The bank or lending institution holding the mortgage on the property requires most if not all of these documents at the closing. These charges and fees add up to about 5 percent of the purchase price of the property.

Current Survey

The survey is a legal description of the property that notes its lot size and boundary lines. A survey team will go to the property and check the boundaries and placement of the house. If the property has been sold in the past couple of years you may be able to save some money by purchasing a certified copy of the survey from the survey company.

Appraisal

An appraisal is an estimate of the value of the property by an expert and confirms for the lender that you haven't paid too much for the property by comparing it with other houses in the neighborhood.

Insurance Binder

The lender also wants confirmation that you will protect the value of the property with an insurance policy. A letter or fax from the insurance broker stating that you have purchased a policy may be all that is necessary. Also, most lending institutions require that they be made a beneficiary of the policy.

Pest Inspection

In most parts of the country, especially in the South, a pest inspection is required. This report states that the property is free of termites or other pests.

Loan Points

The loan points, the fee a lender charges based on a percentage of the loan, will be stated beforehand by the lender. These are payable at closing or in some cases can be added to the loan amount. There may also be an escrow fee for holding the escrow account and processing the paperwork for the loan.

Property Taxes

Property taxes are divided up between the buyer and seller based on the time of year of the transaction. If the seller has already paid for the taxes, the amount is taken from the buyer's account to reimburse the seller.

Title Insurance

Title insurance is used to confirm that the buyer is receiving clear title and ownership. The title company researches the public records and furnishes an abstract confirming free and clear title to the property. In some states a Torrens certificate provides a registration of title to the property. A prepayment of mortgage insurance, if required by the lender, is included in the closing costs.

The Closing

Between when an offer is accepted and the property closing there are several tasks required. A good broker will act as the clearinghouse for these items, but the buyer should be aware of all that's required. Use the checklist in Figure 10.1 to guide you through the process.

Before closing, make arrangements with utility companies that serve the property and have the accounts transferred into your name. The day before or the day of closing, arrange for a final inspection and walk-through of the house and confirm that all systems are in working order.

A typical property closing has all the parties sitting around a large table and signing a pile of papers, most of which were just mentioned. Bring a driver's license to prove who you are, certified checks based on the settlement sheet, and your personal checkbook, just in case there are any last-minute fees required.

A good broker will shepherd you through the process and act as a go-between for you, the loan officer, and the seller's broker. But take the time to review the closing costs and make notes to ask any questions you have. Remember, time is money and you don't want the property settlement delayed, so make sure all the paperwork is being processed. Check with the loan officer about any outstanding issues to settle, and confirm that the insurance company has submitted a copy of your policy. Find out how your checks should be made out (separate or lump sums), and get certified checks for the exact amounts.

Figure 10.1 Buyer's Checklist

TASKS	NOTES	DATE
Order a home inspection of the property		
Review closing cost estimates		
Make money transfers to escrow account		
Order property appraisal		
Order title search		
Consult lender about progress of loan		
Order home insurance		
Order title insurance		
Schedule final walk-through		
Consult with utility companies about changing names on service records		
Review final settlement statement		
Get checks issued for settlement		
Get address of settlement location		

CHAPTER 11

QUICK FIXES, CLEANUPS, AND REPAIRS THAT MAKE YOU MONEY

D o only what shows because buyers are not likely to be impressed by what they can't see. What a prospective buyer does notice is faulty or incomplete workmanship and things that don't work, so spend your time making basic repairs and replacing inexpensive things that show. These improvements tell a buyer that care was given to making the house ready to occupy in move-in condition—just the impression you want to make. Here's our rundown of fast fixes, cleanup chores, and repairs that are easy to do and don't cost a bundle. They add value to the house and make it more salable or rentable.

Decorating

These quick fixes and decorating ideas go a long way to making a house clean, fresh, and inviting. The small investment required for these finishing details makes a house livable and appealing.

Paint

If you do nothing else, paint the rooms. You'll get the best bang for your buck with a $22 gallon of paint because nothing else can make such a dramatic improvement. We use off-white flat latex paint on walls and an eggshell or satin finish on woodwork and trim. By choosing a neutral shade of paint, you give prospective buyers a blank canvas to decorate around. To keep it simple, we paint ceilings and walls the same. Another benefit of painting is the inviting aroma of a freshly painted house.

Window Blinds

For a finished appearance and to eliminate the fishbowl appearance of an empty house, install miniblinds on the windows. For as little as $5 a window you can buy one-inch vinyl miniblinds; the aluminum ones start at around $14 each. An inexpensive vertical blind for a patio door costs about $50. Installing these window treatments is easy, especially because you learn by doing and repeating the process.

Decorative Window Film

If a window is open to the street and a sense of privacy is needed without blocking the daylight, apply a decorative window film that looks like etched glass. It's as simple as cleaning the glass, measuring and cutting the film, and then positioning it on the glass using a squeegee to smooth it in place. You'll find the film sold at home and decorating centers in several designs and patterns.

Floor Registers and Heat Grates

Replace any old units that have rusted or have bent louvers that no longer operate. New registers and grates cost $5 to $10 and are available in a wide range of sizes and shapes. They go a long way toward updating the look and appeal of a room.

Dark Knotty Pine Paneling

Remove the dark finish on old paneling with a gel-type paint and varnish remover. Apply it with a paintbrush and scrape off the finish with a wide putty knife when the remover bubbles and softens. Then clean the paneling with a rubdown of mineral spirits and let it dry. Use an electric finish sander, then vacuum away the dust, and apply a water-base polyurethane with a brush or tung oil with a rag.

Electrical Projects

Here are some inexpensive electrical repairs and replacements that give an old house an updated look. These are basic and easy projects that require a minimum of tools and talents. Learn how to do them yourself so you'll be confident and can do them later on other investment properties.

Electrical Switches and Receptacles

To create a sense of newness and uniformity throughout all the rooms in a house, replace the electrical light switches, receptacles, and plate covers. At about $1 each it's a small investment in an improvement that updates the house. It's a particularly noticeable upgrade if the existing ones have layers of paint or if they are the old push-button type found in many older homes.

To comply with the National Electrical Code, replace each electrical outlet in the kitchen and bathroom with a GFCI—ground fault circuit interrupter. The device reduces the danger of a deadly shock from a faulty plug-in cord or appliance. It measures outgoing and returning current and shuts off the power if it detects a possible dangerous current imbalance. It has a test button that, when it is pushed in, switches off the power to the outlet and any receptacles connected to it. In addition to the kitchen and bathroom, GFCIs are required in all the wet areas of a house such as the laundry room, unfinished basement, garage, outdoor areas, or wherever there's construction activity. It's not difficult to replace a standard receptacle with a GFCI (under $15) or hire an electrical contractor to do it.

Dimmer Switches

Another easy electrical upgrade is to replace a standard light switch in the dining room with a dimmer switch. It's a nice touch that costs about $15 and creates a cozy feeling in a room. The job involves turning off the power at the main circuit panel, removing the old device by disconnecting and cutting the wires, installing the new switch, reattaching the wires to the terminals, testing the device, and finally turning the power back on.

Test the Switches and Receptacles

If the existing switches and receptacles are OK, check to see that they work. Turn on the switches and plug in a small lamp or radio in the receptacles. Make a note of any switches or receptacles that don't work and replace them.

Light Fixtures

In many homes there's a hodgepodge of ceiling light fixtures that, although they may work, are distractions instead of attractions. Assess the style and condition of all light fixtures in the ceilings, and replace those that are dated and worn. Don't go overboard with expensive new ones; for the bedrooms choose a basic $10 ceiling fixture with two bulbs that hugs the ceiling. For a dining room or kitchen choose a traditional style; there's an amazing selection of fixtures in the $40 range at home centers. The same is true for hall lights. Coordinate the hall, dining room, and kitchen fixtures so they are similar in style and finish.

Thermostat

Replace an old thermostat with a new one, especially if it has years of paint around its edges. You'll find a standard round device for about $30 to $40 and a programmable unit for $50 to $100; either one is a noticeable upgrade.

Walls, Doors, and Windows

We all know that when you enter a room your eyes immediately go to the hole in the wall or the broken windowpane. Any eyesore usually draws attention, and that's not the impression you want to make to prospective buyers. These repairs cost next to nothing and can be completed in little time. They're all worth doing.

Wall Repairs

The holes in walls left from pictures and decorations look like nasty pockmarks when the house is emptied out. Before painting walls, spend the time to repair the holes so the finish surface will be flat and smooth. Look for holes in the walls behind doorknobs without the protection of a doorstop and on walls in eating areas behind where a chair was often pushed back and made a dent. Repair the hole in the wallboard and then install a new doorstop.

Use wallboard compound to fill in nail holes. For larger holes in the wall the process is a little more involved. Cut out the damaged area, use a wallboard patch to fill it in, apply wallboard compound, let it dry, and then sand smoothly. The repair costs are less than $20, and a doorstop that screws into the floor molding costs about $1, an inexpensive upgrade.

If there are nail pops, crescent-shaped cracks caused by wallboard pulling away from warped wall studs, you can repair them. Use a nail set to drive the nail tight against the stud and then place a new nail a few inches above the original. Drive the new nail head into the wallboard to hide the nail head and make a slight dimple in the wallboard. Fill the nail head with wallboard compound, let it dry, and then sand smoothly.

Closet Doors

Tune up closet sliding doors so they open and close easily. Lift the door up so its glide wheel comes off the track. Then inspect the rollers along the top, and if they don't turn freely, apply a few drops of household oil. If the ball bearings don't move and the glide wheels are frozen, replace the tracks or glides, each $2 items.

Tune up bifold doors by cleaning the track installed on the top of the doorjamb. Lubricate the track with a spray of silicone so the doors will slide freely. Check that the doorstops on the floor are not bent, loose, or dirty. Replacement guides and hardware are sold in the hardware section of hardware stores and home centers, where you'll find a complete set of bifold-closet-door hardware for $18, a small investment to make the doors operational.

Add lighting to a closet without wiring with battery-operated closet lights. Some of these $6 push on/off fixtures have a hanger for a clothes rack; others are installed on the wall with a backing of a self-stick adhesive.

Exterior Door

Replace an old lock and add a sense of security with a new deadbolt lock for about $35. If you're giving your entry door a face-lift, replace the threshold, too, especially if you have plans to change the carpeting or flooring material. In case you discover uneven surfaces after removing layers of old flooring, choose a threshold that is self-adjusting so that you can even out the surface. The best time to make these improvements is after you paint or finish the door.

Storm/Screen Door

Make an old storm door look new with a $12 screen door handle. The job involves removing the old handle and checking out the holes to see if they can be used for the new handle. If not, use the paper template that comes packaged with the handle as a guide for drilling new mounting holes.

If the pneumatic door closer binds or doesn't operate properly, clean the shaft with an oily rag to remove dirt or rust. Apply a light coating of lithium, also called white grease, to prevent rust and lubricate the seal. Adjust the screw in the end of the piston assembly to make the door close slower or faster. If the closer is too old to adjust, you can replace it with a new one in a few simple steps.

Sliding Patio Door

A patio door may be difficult to open and close because of a buildup of dirt or debris in the track that clogs the lubrication in the rollers. Clean out the track with cotton swabs, and if that doesn't help, replace the old rollers with new track hardware, which costs about $10. You have to remove the door panels, so schedule the job during temperate weather.

Double-Hung Windows

If an old window sash is difficult to slide up and down, lubricate the pulley shafts with a squirt of lubricating oil like WD-40. The pulleys are located at the top of the window jamb where the rope enters the jamb. The lower sash must be closed to expose the pulleys, but the upper sash has to be open to get to them. Use the extension straw of the can to direct the oil into the center of the pulley. The oil helps the wheels turn freely so the window sash can open and close.

Window Glass

You can replace a windowpane in a double-hung window for about $15, which covers the materials. The job involves removing the broken pane and putty and then using new glazing putty and glazier points to secure the replacement glass.

Screens

Anyone can replace old or torn screening with new fiberglass screening fabric. First remove the spline in the groove of the frame, which holds the screening in place. Then replace the screening and secure it with the old spline. If it's brittle you'll need a roll of new spline. Fifteen dollars will buy the material and tools you need.

Windowsills

Two-part epoxy wood filler does a good job of rebuilding damaged wood and lets you shape and sand the surface so it conforms to its original appearance. It's a good choice for fixing a rotten windowsill. The filler system has two parts: a liquid that's squeezed into the damaged sill to stabilize the wood and a pastelike filler applied with a putty knife that hardens and conforms to the shape. When the filler is dry, you sand it smooth and paint it.

Bathroom

Although it's a small room, a bathroom can be dirty with buildup of scum and mildew. It takes time and patience to scrub and scour, but your work will pay off because a dirty bathroom is a definite turnoff to home buyers.

Clean Surfaces

To remove the buildup of soap scum and water marks on chrome bathtub fixtures, use a 50-50 solution of household vinegar and water. Soak a rag in the solution and wrap it around the fixture for a few minutes. Then use the rag to scrub the fixture. You may have to make more than one application for tough stains.

Use a spray cleaner that attacks mildew on all surfaces in the bathroom where mildew has grown. Increase the ventilation in the room to prevent it from returning.

Tile Grout

Apply a new coat of grout around a ceramic tile bathtub surround for a fast face-lift. It's a good idea to protect the tub floor with a heavy drop cloth or cardboard and remove the tub spout and handle faucets first. The job involves removing the old grout with an inexpensive grout saw, cleaning out the seams with the crevice tool of a vacuum, and then applying the new grout. Smooth the joints, wipe away the grout haze, caulk the joints, and then reinstall the fixtures.

Bathtub Caulk

Remove old caulk with a putty knife and clean the joint between the wall and tub and the wall around the sink. Scrub the joint with an old toothbrush to remove dirt and grit. Let the joint dry completely before applying a new silicone sealant or tub caulk, which are easy to apply.

Kitchen

Even if Martha Stewart lived in your home's kitchen (which she probably didn't), go through the cabinets and appliances and scrub and scour them clean. This grunt work will pay off because no one wants to think about moving into a less-than-sparkling kitchen. Troubleshoot the appliances to make sure they're in working order.

Cabinets

Wash the insides of cabinets with a household cleaner. If cabinet pulls or hardware are worn and outdated, replace them with new hardware. To avoid having to drill new holes for new hardware and filling the old holes, bring a sample of the old hardware to the store. Limit your selection of new hardware to ones with installation holes spaced like the old ones.

Cabinet Hinges

Stuffing a wooden matchstick or toothpick with wood glue into the screw hole is one way to repair ill-fitting hinges, but that's a temporary fix. For a permanent repair remove the loose screws and hinges and fill the holes with an epoxy or polyester wood filler mixed with its catalyst. After it has hardened, sand the filler and drill new screw holes to reinstall the hinge.

Range Hood

Turn off the power to the range hood or range if the hood is part of the appliance. Look for the grease filter, which is usually under the hood in front of the blower air intake. Remove the filter and wash it in soapy water. You may need a strong grease-cutting cleaner if the filter hasn't been cleaned recently. Use a scrub brush to remove grease and dirt between the grill louvers, and clean inside of the fan housing and the exterior and interior of the hood. When dry, reassemble the filter and resume power.

Dishwasher

Check to see that the pump screen and spray arm holes are free of small food particles and mineral deposits. The pump screen is usually located in the well at the base of the unit. Scrub the screen with a stuff brush and soapy water. Use a straight pin or thin wire to unclog any holes you can't see through in the spray arm. Clean the exterior of the dishwasher.

Refrigerator

Clean the interior and exterior of the unit with soapy water and then pull it away from the wall so you have access to the condenser coils located on the bottom or back. A buildup of dust and lint prevents the flow of air from inside the unit to the air outside. Use a long-handled snow brush (from your car) to dust off the coils. If the refrigerator has a drain pan at the bottom, clean it thoroughly to remove odors.

Butcher Block

To renew a stained or knife-scarred butcher block, use a hook-type paint scraper with a sharpened blade and an electric palm sander. Protect the surface around the butcher block with a strip of masking tape. Then, following the grain of the wood, press down as you pull the scraper toward you. Use a palm sander with a heavy sandpaper to work on dark stains or burn marks, then use a light sandpaper to finish-sand the surface. Brighten the surface with a sponge and a 50-50 solution of household bleach and water. Then neutralize the bleach with a rag soaked in white vinegar and wash the surface with soap and water. Final-sand the surface with lightweight sandpaper and apply a top finish of a clean rag soaked in mineral oil.

Safety and Efficient Systems

The safety of a house and the efficiency of its systems are important features noted by appraisers, home inspectors, and prospective buyers. Take the time to install the necessary safety equipment and service the systems so the house makes a good impression.

Smoke and CO Detectors

This $30 device measures the concentration of CO (carbon monoxide) and smoke and sounds an alarm when a potentially harmful level is reached. Because the unit is battery-operated, there's no electrical outlet needed. Install one alarm on each level of the house and outside the bedrooms. These detectors are on the list of requirements for insurance, so make sure they're installed when the house is inspected. Home inspectors look for them too.

Heat Pump or Central Air

Trim back any overgrown plants or shrubbery around the unit. While the foliage can shield it from the hot sun and make it more efficient, overgrown bushes can get sucked against the air-intake grill and block the flow of air through the coils.

Furnace

Use a crevice tool of a shop vacuum to clean the area around the blower of the furnace. Measure the size of the furnace filter and buy a new one and replace it.

Radiators

Before the heating season begins, slowly empty or "bleed" the air from the system. Get a small can or bucket to catch the water runoff, and use a radiator key or screwdriver to turn the bleed valve stem counterclockwise about a half-turn or until you hear air hiss out. The bleed valve is located at the top end of the radiator and at one end of the baseboard convector. You may have to remove a cover or open the panel at the end of a baseboard unit to find the valve.

House Exterior

It's easy to forget about the exterior of a house unless you inspect it regularly. Make a favorable impression on everyone who drives by with these basic maintenance chores for the outside of the house.

Gutters and Downspouts

Clean out gutters so rainwater can drain through them and not pool around the foundation of the house. Position a diverter, also called a splash block (about $6 to $10), at the base of each downspout to direct the water away from the house. Seal any leaking joints with silicone caulk. Refasten any hangers and gutters that sag or have pulled away from where they are attached to the house.

Exterior Light and House Numbers

Drive up to the house in the evening when it is dark and see if you can read the address and if the front entry is well lighted. If not, replace the light and get larger house numbers.

Dirty Deck

Sweep the deck and hose it down with the spray nozzle of a garden hose. Then use a scrub brush broom to remove a buildup of dirt. Or rent a power washer to spray-wash the dirty deck. When clean and dry, apply a coat of sealer and repair any loose or broken boards, railing, or stairs. Rake out debris that accumulates beneath the deck.

Brick Efflorescence

Sometimes brick develops a condition called efflorescence, in which mineral salts contained in the brick react with water in the masonry and rise to the surface and evaporate, leaving white blotches that look like dusting powder. To remove it, use a stiff wire brush and a garden hose to wash the surface. Then apply a coat of clear water sealer when the brick is clean and dry.

Find the cause of the excess moisture behind the brick and fix it. It might be a leaking gutter, a loose downspout, or missing caulk around doors and windows that lets water seep behind the brick.

Garage

Clean out the garage and organize anything that's stored there. If lawn tools were left behind by the previous owner, leave only the ones in good condition; get rid of everything else in the garage. Sweep and scrub the floor with a heavy-duty degreaser.

If there's a garage door opener, get fresh batteries for the remote opener and change the lightbulb in the garage.

Blacktop Driveway

If the driveway shows signs of wear, a new topcoat of sealer will improve its appearance, plus maintain it for longer use. Pull the weeds growing alongside the driveway and rake the area so it is neatly edged. Before applying the sealer, sweep the surface and fill in any holes with an asphalt patching compound. Apply the sealer with an old push broom or applicator, spreading it from the garage door and working your way out toward the street. Don't forget to barricade the wet surface and park your car elsewhere while the coating dries.

Landscaping

Second only to putting a new coat of paint on the siding, trimming overgrown and neglected landscaping is an improvement that won't go unnoticed. With a few basic pruning and grooming lawn tools and a lawn mower, you can transform an eyesore into a nicely manicured landscape.

Lawn, Trees, and Shrubs

Maintain the lawn by cutting it on a regular basis. Prune and groom trees and shrubbery by cutting away the excess foliage, dried ends, and heavy branches with pruning shears and loppers. Get advice from a local lawn and garden center about the best time to prune specific trees and shrubbery in your area.

Edging Lawn and Garden Beds

A $20 edging tool and your time pays back with a neatly manicured lawn and garden beds. This is a no-brainer spruce-up that keeps the lawn from invading garden beds. Dig the edger down about six inches into the soil and create a V-shaped trench between the lawn and garden. As you work, remove any weeds and loosen the soil so that it's easy to work with.

Worn Lawn

Reviving a lawn involves removing the weeds, raking and leveling the soil, and adding amendments such as organic matter, fertilizer, lime, or sulfur. Then apply a starter fertilizer and seed and nurture the new seedlings with a steady watering routine.

CHAPTER 12

ESTIMATING FIX-UP COSTS

We hope you'll refer to this chapter often and use it as a quick reference to cost out improvement projects and services for investment property that you're considering. Although these are national average costs, they should give you a benchmark for estimating the expense of bringing a property to its potential value. The cost data is from our weekly newspaper column, "Do It Yourself . . . Or Not?" which has been running since 1987 when we began the database. The do-it-yourself (DIY) cost of projects is based on national average cost data from major retailers in the Northeast, Southeast, Southwest, Midwest, and West/Mountain regions of the country and e-commerce websites with home-improvement products. The pro cost is determined by averaging cost and data information in several construction books that are updated annually and used by contractors to prepare job bids.

To give you more specific cost information, we've included Table 12.1, which lists cost adjustments for many major cities. For example, if you live in and around Chicago, Illinois, the costs given in this chapter should be adjusted by 110.9 percent (national cost × 1.109).

When we analyze the work required for an investment property, we look at the cost of the improvement projects and ask ourselves whether we should do the work or hire out the job. In general, we practically always do the grunt work, which we jokingly refer to as the "mindless tasks" that require little in the way of tools and talents. These are jobs

Table 12.1 Cost Adjustments for Major Cities

City	Percent	City	Percent
Atlanta	88.4	Memphis	85.7
Baltimore	91.6	Milwaukee	101.2
Boston	116.7	Minneapolis	109
Buffalo	102.3	Nashville	85
Chicago	110.9	New Orleans	85.4
Cincinnati	92.5	New York	133.9
Cleveland	101.9	Philadelphia	111.9
Columbus	94.1	Phoenix	90.2
Dallas	86.7	Pittsburgh	102.5
Denver	93.6	San Antonio	83.7
Detroit	104.3	San Diego	107.1
Houston	89.3	San Francisco	124.2
Indianapolis	95.4	Seattle	104.6
Kansas City	98.6	St. Louis	102.7
Los Angeles	110.6	Washington, DC	96

(Source: "Do It Yourself . . . Or Not?", www.diyornot.com)

like removing wallpaper, cleaning out a basement, insulating an attic—all tasks that anyone with a strong back and sense of adventure can successfully perform.

Projects

Many of the houses we work on require upgrades to the electrical and plumbing systems. For these jobs we hire licensed professionals—electricians and plumbers—who will do the job in a workmanlike and timely fashion. When a house requires inspection, we want it to pass with flying colors the first time around, and having seasoned pros has always been a worthwhile investment.

But many jobs are not brain surgery, so a handy investor can do some or all of the work him- or herself. It's sweat equity plain and simple. As you read about the various projects, you'll notice we caution when it's absolutely necessary to hire a pro and when you can do some or all of the work yourself.

Because finding some of these specialists isn't always easy, we include how they are listed in the Yellow Pages, a useful resource for contacting them about specific projects.

The cost of materials and labor is one issue; another is the tools and equipment needed for rehabbing a house. At the end of this chapter you'll find a list of our pet rental tools and why we're fans of our local rental center. But first, let's get started on all the projects you might encounter while rehabbing a house.

Cleaning

Often a house will carry a depressed asking price because it's just plain dirty. A little dirt can be overcome, but when it's combined with mildew and lingering pet and/or smoke odors and the house is filled with furniture and debris, a lot more than elbow grease is needed. General housecleaning services range upward of $15 an hour, and you'll find them listed in the Yellow Pages under "House Cleaning."

They run the gamut from individuals to commercial franchise services. If the house has been neglected and requires more than cleaning, there are specialists in fire damage and restoration who can repair damage and administer antimildew and antibacterial treatments to houses.

Carpet

To clean about 500 square feet of carpeting, a carpet-cleaning service charges about $200. You can rent a rug-cleaning machine for $35 a day, plus $20 more for the cleaning solution. While there's a steep cost difference, consider using a service if the carpeting has stains or pet odors; a do-it-yourselfer can tackle routine cleaning, but for stubborn stains and pervasive odors, it's better to hire a professional. We schedule this work at the end of the job sequence, once all the painting is completed and just prior to putting the house on the market or moving in.

LESSONS LEARNED

To protect freshly cleaned carpeting in a house on the market, we invest in new paper/plastic-backed drop cloths and cut them in strips about 24 inches wide to serve as runners. We lay them down on a path from the front and back doors and throughout the rooms. It's a subtle suggestion for those viewing the house to follow and prevents a trail of dirty, wet footprints on freshly cleaned carpeting. We've been told by realtors that this says a lot about our sense of pride in workmanship.

Power Washing

Outside power washing can transform dirty siding or a mildew-covered deck or patio in a matter of hours. In the Yellow Pages the service is listed as "Pressure Washing," but it is divided into businesses that clean buildings ("Building Cleaning—Exterior") and those that specialize in decks and other outdoor structures ("Cleaning Systems—Pressure, Chemical.")

A service will charge about $420 to clean the exterior of a 2,000-square-foot house, but you can rent a power washer for about $70 a day and do the job yourself if you like working in a *wet* environment (more about rental tools later in this chapter).

If the house is historic or has loose or damaged siding, think seriously about hiring out the job to a specialist because the powerful blast of the unit can be harmful. If the house has two stories, budget more to rent scaffolding so that you can work on the upper level of the house safely.

A power washer is the tool to use to remove mildew and dirt from a deck. After washing the deck, it's a good idea to protect it with a water sealer or repellent.

If cleaning both the siding and a deck are necessary, it's a good bet you can hire a pro to do the job in one day: something to consider if you're looking for an excuse not to do it yourself.

Chimney

A chimney sweep charges $100 to $150 to inspect and clean a typical two-story fireplace chimney, depending on the degree of creosote buildup and whether there's an insert or an oddly shaped flue to work in. Safety experts say a chimney should be cleaned every year to eliminate the buildup of creosote, which can lead to a chimney fire. The investment is a good one, especially if a house is old and you cannot judge the condition of the chimney.

Schedule the cleaning early in a rehab project to keep a cloud of chimney dust and soot from damaging freshly painted walls or clean carpeting. Make sure the hearth is protected with two drop cloths, one on the bottom to protect the floor and the other on top to pick up the soot and debris that falls from the chimney into the hearth.

Roll-Off Containers

When a house is left filled with materials such as old carpeting, appliances, and furnishings, a Dumpster is needed to remove them before you can clean anything. Figure about $250 for the cost of having a small roll-off container or Dumpster delivered and then removed when it's filled. Check with your local landfill to see if there's an additional dumping charge. Also check with the local building department to learn if there are time restrictions or other regulations for having a Dumpster sit in front of a property.

Make sure you're at the property when a Dumpster is delivered so it's positioned correctly. When these monsters are dropped off their truck, they can damage the pavement or ground surface. You should be there to be certain its location isn't infringing on a neighbor's property or damaging the lawn or driveway of your property.

Carpentry

There are many carpentry jobs involved when remodeling or repairing a house, and there are many specialists who perform them. See Table 12.2 for examples of carpentry projects and their costs. A finish or trim

Table 12.2 Costs of Carpentry Projects

Project	Carpenter	DIY
Replace a medicine cabinet	$193	$150
Install 10-foot post-form laminate countertop	$255	$120
Replace five-foot-wide sliding mirror closet door	$200	$135
Install a granite 37-inch-wide vanity countertop	$285	$200
Install a towel bar	$ 75	$ 40
Replace a 24-by-36-inch casement window	$331	$230
Install a 10-by-12-foot suspended ceiling	$240	$145

carpenter has the skills, tools, and experience to install many different materials and components of a house—woodwork and molding, paneling, flooring, shelving and built-ins, doors, and windows. In most cases he or she has come up through the ranks of the trade and evolved using woodworking tools and techniques. Some trim carpenters specialize in old and traditional houses and are adept at re-creating intricate wood trim, which is sometimes necessary when rehabbing.

You'll find a range of prices charged by carpenters, but few of them work for less than $25 an hour. Many general contractors have carpenters skilled at various levels on their staff.

If the carpentry work required amounts to several small jobs, consider hiring a handyperson, a jack-of-all-trades who can evaluate, estimate, and complete small home repairs. You'll usually find them advertised in local newspapers, and they are listed as "Handyman Services" in the Yellow Pages. If there's a bulletin board in a hardware store or home center, you may find postings of their business cards.

Plan to call a handyperson service when you have more than one job because often they charge a minimum fee to cover the expense of traveling, and you should make it worthwhile for you and the handyperson. Make a list of projects so the handyperson can make all the installations and small repairs in one trip. This works out to both your advantages.

Another option for hiring a carpenter is to use the installation service for building materials, appliances, and fixtures offered at many lumberyards and home centers. The turnkey service, created for consumers who don't have the time or can't find references for tradespeople, also works nicely for a real estate investor.

Electrical Work

Some electrical work can be completed by home owners, but most requires a licensed electrician who is responsible for the workmanship and quality of his or her workers. (See Table 12.3 for examples of electrical projects and their costs.) These are high-priced professionals who get between $50 and $80 an hour. Electricians fall in two categories: they are either at the master or the journeyman level. A master is the higher level and is trained and qualified to plan, design, install, and maintain electrical systems. A master electrician knows the National Electrical Code and any state requirements, has passed a test, and has at least two years' experience. A journeyman electrician is licensed by the state to install wiring and equipment. Some states require that a journeyman work with a master electrician.

LESSONS LEARNED

Don't be tempted to hire a freelance electrician or one who works on the weekend at a lower rate. When it comes time for the property to be inspected, if the work is unsatisfactory you won't have much recourse except to hire a licensed pro to redo the work—certainly not a way to cut costs.

You'll find electricians in the Yellow Pages under the "Electrical Contractors" listing. If you have the opportunity to evaluate his or her work before hiring an electrician, here are a few things to look for. Electrical outlets and switch plates should lie flat on the surface of walls and be plumb and square, not tilted. At the service panel, wires and cables should run straight, not be tangled or crossed. In a basement or attic,

Table 12.3 Costs of Electrical Projects

Project	Electrician	DIY
Replace a recessed light	$155	$55
Replace a 32-inch ceiling fan	$222	$150
Replace an eight-foot, four-head low-voltage halogen track lighting system	$163	$110
Replace a porch light	$63	$40

Note that these are replacements, so they can be safely completed by a home owner who has experience working with electrical projects.

check to see that wires are attached firmly to the framing at regular intervals.

As we mentioned earlier, you can use a retailer's installation service when buying electrical fixtures or appliances. The retailer arranges for an electrician to do the installation and is responsible for both the scheduling of the job and, of course, your satisfaction.

Flooring

Although we've always thought a fresh coat of paint can do more than anything to transform the appearance of rooms in a house, new or refinished flooring takes a close second. Together they are a dramatic makeover. Our best experience has been buying all the flooring material for a house from one flooring dealer. We make one trip to the flooring store with all the room measurements and see what's available. The installer likes to make one trip to the house and do all the flooring at the same time. We let the retailer determine how much material is needed and then see what they have on hand. The retailer makes a house call to confirm our dimensions and check out the condition of the floor and subfloor.

Boring can be beautiful. Don't be tempted by a low price on a good-quality fuchsia carpeting or wild patterns of resilient material or tiles.

No matter how good it is or what a great price you can get, wild and crazy colors and patterns in flooring material are a turnoff to buyers.

Other investors like to shop around and find flooring materials at closeouts. We find a dealer who has the material we like and good installers, and we stick with them.

See Table 12.4 for examples of flooring projects and their costs.

Refinishing Floors

When we work on investment property, the flooring choice comes down to keeping the existing flooring and improving it, or replacing it altogether. If the property has hardwood floors we refinish instead of replace them. The houses we've remodeled often had oak floors throughout, and they finish up beautifully in a dark or light finish.

The same is true in older historic homes, where the flooring is usually soft pine that cleans up to a rich golden finish. Unfortunately, sometimes old floors have been painted, and that can be a real challenge but worth the effort.

Speaking of effort, refinishing floors is a job we hire a professional to do. We've tried doing the sanding and refinishing ourselves with only marginal results and found hiring a floor sander is a much better idea.

Table 12.4 Costs of Flooring Projects

Project	Professional	DIY
Sand, stain, and seal 14-by-20-foot room	$566	$200
Install a 10-by-15-foot resilient floor	$705	$460
Install a 14-by-20-foot laminate floor	$1,890	$1,330
Tile a 35-square-foot entrance hall	$249	$150
Install 170 square feet of finished parquet tiles	$1,206	$425
Lay carpeting in a 12-by-14-foot room	$518	$310

Note: these cost estimates are for moderately priced materials. They don't include any repair work or underlayment.

Yes, you can rent a floor sander and do it yourself, but you can also do a lot of damage. The machine is a brute to handle, and there's no place to practice using it. All it takes is one mistake with the machine that gouges the floor and you'll spend any money you may have saved paying a floor specialist to repair it. If you want to do some of the work, do the finishing after the floor has been sanded, but we found that handing the work over to a pro gives us the best results.

Carpeting

When a house doesn't have hardwood floors, we opt for wall-to-wall carpeting to make the rooms look spacious and unified, not to mention attractive and easy to clean. We choose a good-quality, tightly woven nylon carpeting in a neutral color and use it everywhere except high-traffic rooms like a foyer, kitchen, bathroom, and utility area. Wall-to-wall carpeting blankets the rooms, reducing noise and providing comfort and insulation.

LESSONS LEARNED

If you want to do some of the grunt work, remove the old carpeting. This low-skill, labor-intensive job is nasty, but it will save you the labor cost of hiring someone.

Resilient Flooring

For high-use rooms like the kitchen, bathroom, and utility room, we install vinyl resilient flooring that blends with the color of carpeting so when the two surfaces meet there's a visual transition separated only by a threshold that conceals the joint at the doorways. Resilient sheet flooring, sold by the yard in 6- and 12-foot-wide rolls, is a good choice for high-traffic areas because it's a tough and durable material. The installation involves several phases: removing the base shoe molding, inspecting the subfloor, cleaning the subfloor (especially at wall joints where dirt and dust accumulate), planning the layout of the material, cutting it to fit, and then installing. The job is completed with new or reused base shoe molding.

LESSONS LEARNED

Thicker carpet may prevent doors from swinging properly. This requires removing the doors from their hinges, measuring how much to trim from the bottom of the door so it will clear the carpeting, and then cutting that amount off the bottom of the door with a saw.

Plastic Laminates

The new laminate or pre-engineered floors are a popular choice for kitchens and family rooms because they're so good-looking and easy to clean. For an investment property they are also easy to install. These laminates come in planks, squares, and blocks in faux wood, marble, stone, and granite patterns. The tongue-and-groove materials are secured together with glue or they snap together. At about $5 a square foot, the glueless laminates are pricey, double what the glue-down laminates cost. If the material provides the look and feel you want and you plan to live in the house for a while before selling or renting it, you won't go wrong.

Ceramic Floor Tile

Ceramic tile is nice material to use in a foyer or entrance hall. A ceramic floor entry provides a durable surface for dirty shoes and snowy boots, yet it can be cleaned easily. When a property is on the market, lay a throw rug on the tiles and it can withstand traffic, not only of prospective buyers but of the team of inspectors and appraisers who eventually have to tour the house. Its hard surface is also a good choice in a bathroom.

When considering a tile floor, choose a neutral color and pattern that blends well with the adjoining floor surfaces, and make sure you are looking at floor, not wall tile, which is thinner and not slip-resistant. A tile floor is installed with thinset adhesive over a sound subfloor that is level and solid. The joints are sealed with grout to complete the installation.

Most foyers and bathrooms are small spaces, so choose tiles scaled to the space. If you're shopping at a flooring center or retailer, you'll find a good selection of floor tiles, which you can put together with carpeting or other materials you'll be using in the house.

If you are prospecting for a tile installer and inspecting his or her work, take an overview of the tiles to see if the surface is level and the tiles appear balanced and symmetrical. The band of tiles outlining the floor should be about the same size around the room. The grout lines should be straight and even and have consistent spacing, and the grout should be in the grooves, not on the tiles.

Parquet Tiles

On occasion we've used 12-inch-square prefinished parquet tiles in an entrance; they provide a complementary contrast to adjoining rooms with carpeting. The tiles can be installed over a smooth, old wood floor that's been sanded smooth with any old paint, lacquer, wax, or shellac removed. Old resilient or sheet flooring must be removed and the floor covered with underlayment before parquet tiles are laid.

Underlayment

The key to a good flooring installation is the underlayment or subfloor underneath the material that provides a smooth, level, uniform surface. The material comes in four-by-eight-foot sheets in thicknesses from ⅛ inch to ¾ inch, the thicker being the most common. Hardboard underlayment is used over wood or plywood subfloors to bridge gaps and cracks in the floor. Another type of underlayment is frequently used under carpeting, tile, and vinyl flooring. Particle board, the least expen-

sive of these materials, is an engineered material made of wood particles bound together with resin.

Sometimes in a bathroom, we've had to replace the subfloor because
we discovered it was damaged from a water leak in the toilet—this
became obvious only when the toilet or floor was removed. Water had
seeped beneath the floor over time, and the particle board beneath it
had deteriorated.

LESSONS LEARNED

Different floor levels can be an issue and a safety hazard that
causes tripping when you walk from one height floor to another.
If your plans call for installing a new floor on top of an existing
one, make sure you take that into account. It may require
removing a layer of flooring material to bring it down to the
same height as the floor in an adjoining room.

Landscaping

In our experience, most of the landscaping work required on investment
property involves either planting a few shrubs or removing years of overgrown weeds and plantings. In either case we think of the landscaping,
especially at the front of the house, as a way to enhance curb appeal. See
Table 12.5 for examples of landscaping projects and their costs.

Our approach is to spend the minimum required and to work with
what's there. We replace bushes when needed, trim branches of a
sprawling tree, and remove what's overgrown. When it comes to plants,
the standard investment we make is a large clay pot container filled with
colorful flowers along with a new welcome mat.

Often a neglected property is one that's ripe for rehabbing, so we've
had our share of "jungle houses," the term of endearment we use for
those that are totally overgrown with weeds and vegetation. Usually we
can tackle the work, but if the yard is large and time is of the essence,

Table 12.5 Costs of Landscaping Projects

Project	Landscaper	DIY
Remove a two-foot-wide tree stump	$159	$75
Edge a 32-foot garden bed with aluminum edging	$165	$60
Revive a 100-square-foot patch of lawn	$96	$50
Seed a 3,000-square-foot lawn	$230	$190
Plant a 10-foot honeysuckle hedge	$193	$82

we'll hire a landscaper who can come in with a crew and get things cut back and in control.

With an overgrown landscape, concentrate on trimming and nurturing what's there and removing what shouldn't be. If you want to participate in the work, landscaping offers an opportunity because it's a good example of grunt work. Garden tools are inexpensive and you probably already own some. For more heavy-duty projects like removing an eyesore of a tree stump, you'll need to rent a power grinder and a vehicle to transport it.

When a lawn is overgrown and patched with weeds, a few hours with a good lawn mower and trimmer can work wonders. Clumps of weeds, bare spots, and areas of compacted soil are repairable conditions that take time and patience and a few basic lawn tools—more opportunities for a do-it-yourselfer. Any work to renew a lawn and garden should be followed by a routine of watering.

In general, a landscaping service or individual charges about $15 to $20 an hour, depending on the scope of work. You'll find business cards of independents who do yard work posted on the bulletin boards at local lawn and garden centers and see their advertisements in local newspapers in the classified ads or in the home section. A landscape service is a company that does a variety of gardening installations and maintenance work and is listed in the Yellow Pages under "Landscape Contractors."

The landscaping season depends on the climate where you're investing, and the weather conditions can either help or hinder your work. Monsoon rains will keep you from landscaping work, as will a drought that produces soil that's hard as clay. So in some cases you can plan the work in the yard, but Mother Nature will control when you do it.

Painting

Painting, the number one do-it-yourself project, will make the most dramatic improvement to a house, investment or otherwise. We like to paint the interior of a house, so we always do it ourselves. (See Table 12.6 for examples of painting projects and their costs.) We usually hire a painting contractor to paint the exterior siding and trim because it usually requires scaffolding and a lot of ladder work. Inside we paint all rooms (walls and ceilings) in an off-white latex flat paint and use alkyd-based satin enamel on the woodwork and trim and in the bathroom. We buy the paint in five-gallon pails and use rollers and brushes.

We use a gray or beige latex paint in basements, sometimes using a roller, other times renting an airless spray gun, which we found does an amazing job of transforming a dirty and dingy space into a clean and usable one. If needed, we use a floor and porch enamel on the floor with a roller on a pole.

Painting Cover-Ups

If kitchen or bathroom cabinets need a face-lift, we paint them with an oil-based enamel after thoroughly sanding and preparing the surface. We use the same process to conceal ugly wall tile—plastic or ceramic— as long as the tile is sound and not in direct contact with water, like inside a shower or bathtub. And when we find a room with walls covered with dark paneling, we refinish or paint them. There's a real savings when you paint cabinets, wall tiles, or paneling compared with the alternative of removing or replacing them. The key to the cover-up is preparing the surface and priming it so the paint has a smooth surface to adhere to.

For example, wash the surface with a 50-50 solution of household ammonia and water to remove soap film from bathroom walls or grease from kitchen walls. Then use a power sander with 120-grit sandpaper, wood filler, and an alkyd (oil-based) primer. Fill in any nail holes or

Table 12.6 Costs of Painting Projects

Project	Painting Contractor	DIY
Paint walls and ceiling of 12-by-20-foot room	$235	$70
Paint 10-foot wood kitchen cabinets	$185	$75
Paint 20-by-20-foot masonry basement walls with roller	$297	$90
Paint siding and trim of 2,500-square-foot house	$1,233	$550
Paint 400-square-foot porch floor	$131	$45
Remove varnish from two double-hung windows and doors	$195	$30
Remove two layers of paint from one double-hung window	$127	$35

blemishes in cabinets or paneling with wood filler, and when it's dry, sand the surface smooth. For knots in the paneling, use a spray stain blocker like B-I-N so there won't be any bleed-through of the stain.

This is another good example of grunt work that yields a high return on your investment.

Plumbing Work

Most of the plumbing work in an investment property should be done by a licensed plumber because many local building codes require it, and in the end everything must pass inspection. Plumbers charge between $60 and $80 an hour for small projects. They usually work for less on major projects.

That said, there are several repairs or upgrades a handy investor can make, if he or she has some plumbing experience and the time it takes to complete them. Plumbing isn't brain surgery, but it's not that simple either. Most plumbing replacements such as a faucet or garbage disposal don't require a building permit and are so straightforward that a handy person can do it. See Table 12.7 for examples of plumbing projects and their costs.

You'll find plumbers listed in the Yellow Pages as "Plumbing Contractors," and from their ads you'll be able to see what the scope of their work is. Just as with electricians, you can get an "installed price" at a retailer and have plumbing fixtures installed.

Table 12.7 Costs of Plumbing Projects

Project	Plumber	DIY
Replace a showerhead with a slide bar	$175	$95
Replace a 40-gallon electric water heater	$471	$250
Replace a dishwasher	$710	$600
Replace a washerless bathroom faucet	$131	$85
Install a porcelain pedestal sink	$704	$450
Replace a single-bowl, 25-inch-wide stainless sink and faucet	$343	$250
Replace a garbage disposal	$286	$100
Replace a toilet	$295	$180
Replace a single-lever washerless cartridge-type kitchen faucet	$117	$95
Replace a pedestal sink	$704	$450
Replace a ½ hp sump pump	$195	$95

Wallboard

Wallboard, the material that makes up the walls of houses built after the 1950s, is a commodity item sold in 4-by-8- or 4-by-12-foot sheets or panels. It is heavy to lift and time-consuming to install. See Table 12.8 for examples of wallboard projects and their costs. Wallboard panels have a paper facing over a gypsum plaster core. The panels are screwed or nailed to wall studs, and the joints between them are covered with fiberglass or paper tape and then embedded in compound. The compound is sanded smooth, and another application is made to fill in the voids and create a smooth, seamless surface. It's sanded again and then primed and painted. When painted, the paper facing of the wallboard absorbs some of the paint and dries to a smooth surface.

In an investment property, wallboard is most often used to create a room where there wasn't one, such as an attic expansion, or as a replacement to repair damaged wallboard. The most common type used in houses is ½- and ⅝-inch-thick wallboard.

There are also specialty types of wallboard. Foil-backed wallboard is used on exterior walls and in high-moisture areas like a bathroom to provide a vapor barrier. Green board also is used in high-moisture

Table 12.8 Costs of Wallboard Projects

Project	Drywall Contractor	DIY
Hang wallboard in a 15-by-20-foot room	$1,276	$300
Repair damaged wallboard	$62	$16

areas, and it's the preferred backing for ceramic tile, when not in a tub or shower stall. Cement board—a ½-inch-thick board with a cement base, instead of plaster—is waterproof and was created as a base for tile in wet areas.

Wallpaper

Selecting colors and patterns of wallpaper is a very personal choice, so spending a lot of money on it isn't the best investment you can make. See Table 12.9 for examples of wallpaper projects and their costs. If you wallpaper any room, make it the kitchen or bathroom, but if you do, choose very neutral colors and patterns. For the best results use a vinyl-coated, fabric-backed, and prepasted wall covering that is durable, pliable, and easy to hang. To estimate the cost of doing a room, figure that a double roll will cover approximately 56 square feet and cost about $45. You'll find both cheaper and much more expensive options, but that's a ballpark figure to work with.

A less expensive way to add a spark of color to a room is with a wallpaper border, which does a nice job of defining the space in a kitchen or bathroom without overpowering it.

Removing Wallpaper 101

We save a lot of money removing wallpaper, a tedious job that's the ideal kind of grunt work for the not-so-handy investor. Tape plastic drop cloths to the baseboard molding around the room to protect the floor. This does double duty when the job's over. The messy wet scraps of wallpaper are on the drop cloth so you untape it, wrap it up, and throw it away.

Table 12.9 Costs of Wallpaper Projects

Project	Paperhanger	DIY
Hang wallpaper in a 14-by-18-foot room	$650	$275
Hang a double border (at ceiling and chair rail) in 12-by-14-foot room	$165	$70
Remove two layers of painted wallpaper in 14-by-18-foot room	$327	$25

You need a razor scraper, a Paper Tiger (a scoring tool), and a quart of wallpaper remover. You'll also need a bucket and paint roller to wet down the walls. Score the walls with the Paper Tiger, which penetrates the wallpaper without damaging the surface of the wall behind it. Then apply the remover with the roller so it gets behind the paper to loosen the adhesive holding the paper to the wall. Use the razor scraper to scrape the paper off the wall.

Or, instead of chemical wallpaper remover, you can use a wallpaper steamer. You will still use the Paper Tiger to create tiny holes in the wallpaper so the steam can penetrate the paper. Fill the steamer's tank with water, plug it in, and when the water begins to boil, steam comes out of the hot plate. As you hold the hot plate to the wall with one hand, you use a wide putty knife or razor scraper in the other to remove the wallpaper.

Wall Tiling

Ceramic tile is a tough, hardworking material ideal for covering walls, and we've used it primarily on the three walls surrounding a bathtub. It comes in virtually any color and countless styles, but we usually choose the most basic neutral shades. You can find tile contractors in the Yellow Pages under the listing "Tile-Ceramic—Contractors and Dealers." You can also get an installed price for tile work from many tile retailers and home centers where tile is sold. See Table 12.10 for examples of wall tile projects and their costs.

Table 12.10 Costs of Wall Tile Projects

Project	Tile Contractor	DIY
Tile three walls of a bathtub surround	$362	$155
Tile eight square feet of a kitchen backsplash	$198	$130

If you have more than one tiling project for a property, definitely schedule the work for all of them at the same time so the tiling contractor can minimize his or her return visits. Tiling work involves several phases. First, the walls are prepared and patched (if necessary), and then the layout of the tiles is planned. Next, the mastic is applied and the tiles are laid. When the tiles have set, then all the spaces between the tiles are filled with grout. When set, the tiles are washed off and the grout is scored.

Tools and Equipment: To Rent or to Own?

If you're a real estate investor working on houses to improve them for resale or rent, you can rationalize buying designer power tools. No one (not even the IRS) will question your logic. There are some specialty tools we use infrequently, so we rent them; others that we use regularly, we buy.

Airless Paint Sprayer (Rent)

When we have a large basement with rough walls to paint, we rent an airless sprayer that pumps paint through a small hole in the tip of a spray gun at very high pressure. We've found spraying walls, despite the intensive preparation time to mask surfaces you don't want to paint, is a good bet.

Long Ladders and Scaffolding (Rent)

We don't have a good place to store long ladders and scaffolding so we rent them when they're needed, which is usually for painting. We like A-frame ladders, which are self-supporting and adjustable for painting stairwells and working on ceilings.

Heat Gun (Own)

For less than $75 you can buy your own heat gun and you'll find it useful for any number of occasions. It's good for removing paint and varnish, most definitely, but it comes in handy when you're unfreezing frozen water pipes in the winter and removing adhesive on a floor after the tiles have been popped off.

Tile Saw (Own)

You can rent or borrow a tile saw wherever you buy tile, but we bought one to always have it available, and it's proved to be a good $100 investment. We do small tiling projects like around bathtubs and sometimes a backsplash, and we like the convenience of always having a saw available that makes clean, accurate cuts. Because it's not rented out, we don't have to worry about misaligned cutters or dull blades.

Wallpaper Steamer (Own)

We've taken off more rolls and layers of wallpaper than we care to remember and prefer to own rather than rent a steamer. Granted, the rental units are for commercial use so they're bigger and beefier, but the consumer-grade unit that costs about $50 works just fine to loosen the paper's adhesive so it can be scraped off the wall.

CHAPTER 13

SPACE-EXPANDING POSSIBILITIES

The rooms in a house that are under roof offer the best potential for expansion because they are already part of the structure. An attic has an existing roof and floor, a basement is enclosed by the existing structure, and a back or side porch is an unfinished annex just waiting to be enclosed. Improving these spaces doesn't require expensive new foundation work or building exterior walls; instead, it's a matter of reusing the space to its optimum advantage. Therein lies the challenge: knowing when a room offers untapped potential living space and when it should be left as it is.

Of course, there are limiting factors to consider. The joists and framing of the attic, no matter how large, might not be constructed to withstand the load of additional living space; that basement may be plagued with dampness. And an open porch, while tempting to enclose and convert, might add more architectural character and value to the house than an enclosed space would. In this chapter we'll look at how to recognize expansion possibilities in the attic, basement, and porch and when and how to tap their potential.

Converting an Unfinished Attic

Converting an unfinished attic takes advantage of the existing foundation, walls, roof, and siding. Finishing the space requires the basic carpentry skills of framing, insulating, and hanging wallboard and trim. To assess an attic, the first thing we look for is what we call an "easy convert," or a wide-open unfinished space that can be transformed into rooms. The addition of bedrooms and a bathroom can reinvent a two-bedroom, one-bath house to one with four bedrooms and two baths, a dramatic upgrade. The next best possibility is to convert an attic to usable, accessible storage space, a feature that's on every home owner's or renter's wish list.

Many bungalow- and Cape Cod–style homes were built with unfinished attics to attract budget-strapped home owners who could finish off the attic when their time and bank accounts allowed. These one-story, 1920s-vintage homes typically have steep roofs framed with rafters and ceiling joists and were designed with a living room, dining room, kitchen, bathroom, two or three bedrooms, and a stairway leading to an unfinished attic. That stairway and unfinished attic offer a tremendous opportunity to reinvent the house.

LESSONS LEARNED

If the house has a low-pitch roof like a ranch or an attic with crisscrossing two-by-fours, which indicate the roof has truss construction, forget about expansion possibilities because neither are designed for living space.

Attic Inspection

You can make a general inspection of the attic at the same time you inspect it for conversion possibilities. Bring a flashlight, a 25-foot measuring tape, and a clipboard with paper to make a rough sketch of the space and jot down your findings.

Begin by looking at the attic ceiling or sheathing, which is actually the underside of the roof. Look for signs of any sagging areas and damage from insects, rot, or condensation. Pay particular attention to roof penetrations like the plumbing vent and the chimney, where leaks may occur. Sometimes what looks like water damage is actually condensation due to inadequate ventilation. Look for vents and see if they are screened to deter animals from entering.

Depending on your geographic location, there are specific government recommendations and local building code requirements for the R-value—the insulating power—of roof and wall insulation. Six inches of attic insulation used to be considered enough, but in most parts of the country today, 12 inches is considered the minimum.

If there are recessed lighting fixtures in the ceilings of rooms below the attic, inspect the fixtures. First, go downstairs to look at the fixture in each room to find out its rating. An IC-rated fixture can be completely covered with insulation, but a non-IC- or T-rated recessed fixture must be at least three inches away from insulation. Also look for bathroom vents to see if they go to the outside. Look at electrical wiring to see that it is not damaged or spliced.

For expansion possibility, look beyond the basics.

Access

The location of the stairs is a prime factor that determines whether an attic has living space potential. For aesthetics, the best location is in the center of the house or off the main living or dining area, not a hidden stairway tucked at the back of the house. A centrally placed stairway provides easy access from the main living area.

A stairway location also determines the floor plan of the attic makeover. The best layout usually includes a central hall and landing where there's access to all the rooms. There's nothing worse than tandem rooms lined up one after the other like railroad cars. A hall with doors leading to bedrooms and bathroom make all the rooms on the second floor accessible and private so no one has to go through a room to get to another one.

Yes, it's possible to relocate back stairs to another part of the first floor, but it's an expensive option that requires major structural changes. Instead, keep the stairs at the back of the house and use the attic as a storage area. The exception here is if the home is grossly undervalued for its neighborhood. In that case, totally redesigning the floor plan and moving the stairs might make sense.

In many homes, the staircase leading to an unfinished attic separates a dining room and kitchen and opens into the kitchen. In that case, you can open up the stairway and reroute the stairs so they open into the dining room instead, which makes the staircase more formal and appear to have always been there. Close off the doorway to the stairs in the kitchen and gain more wall space there. Open the wall in the dining room and create a raised landing finished with a balustrade and wood-work that match the existing moldings and trim. This detail enhances the entire house and ties the staircase into the design of the home.

Building codes require that stair treads must be a minimum of 10 inches and stair risers a maximum of 7¼ inches. The headroom must be no less than 80 inches, measured vertically from the finished floor at the landings.

The codes also require a second stairway or window as a means of escape. For this an egress/rescue window should be included in the plan for the conversion. This type of window, which allows for a convenient exit in the event of a fire, must have a maximum opening of at least 20 inches wide by 24 inches high, have a maximum sill height of 44 inches, and be operated without keys or tools. When installed at the correct height above the floor, some roof windows meet these requirements.

Floor Joists

Attics that are not designed for future conversions may have floor joists, actually the ceiling joists of the rooms below, that are too small to sup-port a living area. Depending on the size of the rooms below, the attic floor joists must be at least two-by-sixes and possibly larger. Large rooms require larger floor joists because they must span long distances without additional support. Generally, if the attic floor has two-by-six joists or larger joists and the span between the load-bearing walls on the floor below does not exceed 10 to 12 feet, the floor is strong enough to support a living area and we consider the space a candidate for remodeling.

Ask the local building department or a contractor or refer to a build-ing codebook to determine the load factor. To support only the ceiling, the load is 10 pounds per square foot of the rooms below. For attic storage, the load is 20 pounds per square foot, and for a live load of people and furniture, the load is 30 to 40 pounds per square foot.

Building codes involving attic conversions are precise about joist size as it relates to the space between load-bearing walls. Before applying for a building permit, find out what the requirements are so you can be sure that your plan will comply. In some cases the building department will require an engineer-architect to draw up and stamp the plan.

Headroom

We found that a house with good access to a second floor and adequate headroom in the attic was built to support future expansion. The International Residential Code for one- and two-story dwellings requires that all habitable rooms, except bathrooms and kitchens, be no fewer than seven feet high. Some codes require seven and one-half feet.

This underscores the importance of learning the requirements from the building department in the town or jurisdiction where a house is located. In some cases, sloped and flat ceilings lower than seven feet high are allowed, but the floor spaces under them that are fewer than five feet aren't considered as part of the calculation of minimum room size.

When measuring the height of the attic space, keep in mind that you have to allow for furring strips, insulation, and wallboard to finish the ceiling and walls.

Fire Blocking

To contain the spread of fire through a concealed draft opening, a fire barrier between floors is required. Approved unfaced fiberglass insulation and lumber is used to fill any gaps between a chimney and floor and ceiling as part of the framing stage of construction. These materials should be measured into the equation.

Lighting, Heating/Cooling, and Ventilation

When assessing an attic for conversion, don't forget to consider lighting the space and providing adequate temperature control and ventilation. Skylights and roof windows are obvious solutions. Consider tapping into the existing heating and cooling systems and adding ventilation, especially if a bathroom is part of the redesign. Thinking of all these considerations at the first inspection and appraisal will help you create comfortable and valuable living space.

Strictly-for-Storage Attics

Sometimes the only access to an attic is a small panel in the ceiling, and it's often tucked away in a closet; if that's the case, it's guaranteed not to be designed for living space. You can replace the panel with a foldaway staircase, which is a more user-friendly way to access the attic for storing items. The unit, which is sold at lumberyards and home centers, comes in a range of ceiling heights from 8 to 10 feet. The stairway is bolted into a rough opening and then trimmed with molding and painted for a finished look on the ceiling. The heavier the unit, the better.

A carpenter will charge about $550 to install a good-quality foldaway staircase, so it's a sizable investment. But don't underestimate the value of storage space in a home. If other houses in the same neighborhood or price range have accessible storage space, adding foldaway stairs to untapped storage space is worth considering.

If you decide to add a unit, rethink its location. It doesn't have to be where the small panel is located. Get a contractor to inspect the attic and its ceiling joists and suggest the best location for one. Ideally, the

LESSONS LEARNED

In an attic without flooring, the storage space is limited to balancing boxes and items across the span of the floor joists. To upgrade the storage capability, consider adding plywood sheets or tongue-and-groove panels laid over the floor joists and secured with wood screws.

stairs will unfold into a room or hallway and be easily accessible to anyone using it.

Use the worksheet in Figure 13.1 when inspecting an attic to take notes and review when you're making a decision about whether to expand it.

If the opening to the attic is narrow, cut the four-by-eight-foot plywood sheets in half vertically so they measure two by eight feet and will fit through the opening. Or use StorageBords, which are two-by-four-foot panels. For less than $100 you can buy the panels for an eight-foot-square area and improve the storage space considerably.

Figure 13.1 Attic Worksheet

NOTES

Stairs

Width of steps _____

Headroom in stairway _____

Open or enclosed _____

Location in house _____

Adjoining walls _____

Location in attic _____

Headroom

At the roof peak or highest dimension _____

At the lowest sidewall _____

Floor Plan of Living Space

Length and width of floor space _____

Length and width of floor space with
 five feet of headroom _____

Dimensions of Floor Joists

Length and width   _____

Insulation

Type and R-value (if any) in ceiling   _____

Type and R-value or depth (if any)
   in floor   _____

Insulation around recessed can
   light fixtures   _____

Location of Permanent Fixtures

Chimney   _____

Electrical wires   _____

Plumbing lines   _____

Heating ducts   _____

Built-in shelving   _____

Other things   _____

Flooring

Open, no finished floor   _____

Plywood sheathing or planks   _____

Attic Ceiling or Sheathing

Rafters   _____

Sagging areas   _____

Signs of pest infestation or rot   _____

Moisture or condensation, fungus   _____

Vents   _____

Basement Conversions

You can take advantage of what a basement has to offer—walls, ceiling, and a floor—and transform it into usable living space. As an investor, it is wise to create just the finished space rather than divide it into rooms for specific functions. Let the owner customize it; you just provide a clean, finished space that is very appealing to a buyer. Separate the finished space with a partition wall for the furnace and other utilities and laundry facilities if they're there, but don't do anything more than that.

Improvements that increase living space add value to the property. We do always clean up the basement and sometimes remodel it. In the case of a small house we feel the additional living space can return more value than the costs. But this holds only if the costs are carefully controlled. Creating a fancy basement family room will not pay off, but transforming a dingy basement into a clean, attractive, usable area will.

Basement Inspection

To consider finishing a basement, make an inspection to determine if it's suitable. Look at the foundation and walls for signs of seepage through small cracks, or a white powdery residue called efflorescence, or indications of mold or mildew. All of these telltale signs indicate that more than paint is needed. The fix might be as easy as cleaning the gutters so rainwater can flow through them and away from the foundation with the simple addition of a downspout diverter to solve the problem. Also, inspect several areas of the cement floor looking for cracks and signs of moisture. If you find chronic signs of moisture or cracks and crevices, call in a waterproofing specialist for a diagnosis.

Stairwells and Windows
If there is an exterior stairwell with concrete stairs, look to see if they are solid or cracked. If there's a drain, does it work? Window wells should be free of water and debris, and the basement windows should open easily and not show signs of wood rot.

Electrical Wiring

Look at the electrical wiring. It should be grounded and show no signs of damage or splices. Be concerned about wires that go nowhere. Basements should have three-prong and GFCI receptacles. They provide shock protection at electrical receptacles by cutting the power almost instantly when they detect a possible dangerous current imbalance. Also look at any lighting fixtures and find their switches.

Plumbing

Inspect the plumbing lines to see if they are copper, plastic, or galvanized, and notice how the lines are connected and secured to ceiling rafters. Metal strapping should be tight and secure. Be sure to find the main water line and see if there is a shut-off valve or a check valve or an anti-backflow device.

And look for the drain lines that take water out of the house. See how they are connected, and look for signs of leaks. Look at the sump pump and trip the float rod to test it. When you lift the rod the motor should start.

Insect Problems

Look to the exposed joists in the ceiling for signs of rot or pest infestation. Termites are a potential problem in most parts of the United States. A professional termite inspection is required in many parts of the country in order to get financing.

Appraising a Basement for Living Space

To determine if a basement is suitable for living space, first look at two key issues: moisture and ceiling height.

Moisture

By their very nature concrete walls and floors that make up the foundation of a house draw moisture from the ground at varying degrees. Small amounts of moisture or condensation that forms on concrete walls can be managed with a dehumidifier. Two solutions to handle larger amounts of moisture are installing a sump pump cut into the floor or digging drainage ditches with gravel and installing drain lines around the high sides of the foundation. Don't consider any improvements to a basement without first removing the source of moisture. And give any property second thoughts if there are signs of serious water problems in the basement.

Ceiling Height

To finish off a basement for living space, most building codes require the ceiling height to be at least 90 inches, which is seven and one-half feet. Because most basements in older houses were not built with finishing in mind, heating ducts, plumbing lines, and electrical wires were installed where it was easy to work on them. When finishing the basement takes priority, the utilities must remain accessible and convenient for repair work but concealed for aesthetics.

Enter the suspended or drop ceiling, a solution for all seasons. A suspended ceiling consists of metal channels that run the length of a room with cross runners and ribs that create a grid for two-by-two-foot or two-by-four-foot acoustical panels that slip into place. This type of ceiling is an ideal way to cover up utilities yet provide access to them because while the channels are permanently fastened to ceiling joists, the panels are easily removed. Another component of a suspended ceiling system is recessed lighting, which illuminates the room with overall lighting without taking up valuable space overhead.

Another way to hide the web of utility lines and furnace ducts is by boxing them in with soffits made of wood framing covered with wallboard. Even easier is to fool the eye and just paint them the same color as the ceiling and walls. Any of the service lines and pipes can be removed and rerouted in a basement ceiling, but it's extremely expensive. For investment purposes, consider only concealing them, not relocating them.

Basement for Storage

The best bang for the buck in a basement is cleaning it, emptying it, and painting it—period. A potential buyer can envision how they'll finish the room or see it as a ready-made storage area, and in either case, it's an appealing feature.

Use a shop vacuum to suck out dust and dirt, especially cobwebs hidden in the ceiling and behind heating ducts and plumbing pipes. Remove any and all debris that's left in the basement. Use a power washer to clean the walls and floor (if necessary).

Deal with any moisture issues by finding the source of the problem and making the necessary repair. Turn on a dehumidifier to remove the dampness.

Paint the walls with a good latex paint with a sprayer or roller. Use a good floor and porch paint to coat the floor, being careful to cut in the paint where the floor meets at the bottom of the walls.

Walls and Support Poles

Wallboard, also called Sheetrock or gypsum board, is the best way to finish basement walls. Wallboard installed over concrete should have a barrier between to eliminate any condensation. Many contractors isolate damp concrete walls with one inch of extruded polystyrene insulation and a layer of six-mil polyethylene. This type of vapor barrier prevents trapped moisture behind the walls.

Stack pipes and support poles located in the center of a basement can be a challenge to conceal. You can't remove them, but you can conceal them. A low-budget solution is to camouflage them with a rope wrap to soften their appearance. Choose a thick natural rope or braided boat dock line and wrap and glue the pole with it beginning at the bottom and working to the top. A more costly but attractive solution is to conceal a support pole as a column, an architectural feature of the room. Have a carpenter build a column around it with collar blocks to anchor and support side panels made of plywood. Trim the top and bottom with molding, and paint it to match the walls.

Floors and Stairs

To create a floating laminate floor system that is built up and not directly attached to the slab, some contractors suggest using polyethylene, rigid-foam insulation over one-by-three sleepers and tongue-and-groove plywood. However, this raises the floor, which can conflict with an already low ceiling or create an issue with the distance between the floor and the first stair riser. We usually use carpeting with a good pad underneath it.

A staircase should have a sturdy handrail secured to a wall and provide safe footing. There should be a five-inch or less gap between vertical balusters and the stair treads, and risers should be safe and well built, whether they are open or closed.

For stairs, most building codes call for a minimum of 7¾ inches for stair risers and 10 inches for treads. We've had the best luck by carpeting enclosed stairs and painting open wooden stairs.

Windows

Windows in basements let daylight in, but at the same time they can create a security breach if the glass can be broken. Consider replacing any old windows with basement hopper windows with either double-pane insulating glass or double-insulated acrylic block panels.

If there is no outside exit from a basement, an egress window—that is, one large enough for a person to get out in case of an emergency—is often required. Some older homes were built before there were any egress window requirements, so ask the building inspector about the code.

Climate Control

Talk to an HVAC (heating, venting, and air-conditioning) contractor to find out if the existing heating, ventilating, and air-conditioning system can be used in the basement. The contractor can tell if the system can

---

LESSONS LEARNED

You know the story about the guy who built the boat in his basement and couldn't get it out? Well, the reverse of that is getting cumbersome building materials inside. Spend time mapping out a strategy to schedule the arrival and delivery of materials, especially bulky ones like wallboard and carpeting.

---

handle the additional square footage or if an additional system will be needed. Most basements are easy to heat and usually have some duct already installed. The pipes running through the basement from the hot-water-heating systems usually provide adequate heat for the space there. Don't enlarge a well-functioning heating or cooling system just to accommodate the basement. But if the system requires upgrading anyway, consider upsizing it to accommodate the basement.

Use the worksheet in Figure 13.2 when inspecting a basement to take notes and review when you're making a decision to expand it.

Figure 13.2 Basement Worksheet

NOTES

Exterior Stairwells

Drain _____

Cracked stairs _____

Window wells

Free of water and debris _____

Foundation and Walls

Signs of seepage through small cracks _____

Efflorescence or a white powdery
    residue _____

Mold or mildew _____

Interior Stairs

Handrail secured to a wall _____

Five-inch or less gap between vertical
    balusters _____

Open or closed stair treads and risers _____

Floor

Cracks in cement floor or slab _____

Sump Pump

Free of water and debris   _____

Test by pulling up the float rod   _____

Ceiling Joists

Signs of rot or pest infestation   _____

Electrical Wiring

Wires that go nowhere   _____

Spliced or damaged wires   _____

Grounded wires   _____

GFCIs   _____

Three-prong receptacles   _____

Lighting Fixtures

Location and switches   _____

Plumbing Lines

Type of water lines (copper, plastic,
galvanized)   _____

How the lines are connected   _____

How the lines are secured to ceiling
rafters (metal strapping)   _____

Main Water Line

Location   _____

Shut-off valve   _____

Check valve or anti-backflow device   _____

Drain Lines

Locations   _____

How they are connected   _____

Signs of leaks   _____

Enclosing a Porch

On older homes many porches were designed to provide an extra out-door space for use during warm weather in the northern climates and during the cool, breezy season in the South. It was a temporary room, sometimes enclosed with screens or windows, often an open portico to catch the breeze and provide a shaded retreat from the sun. Over the years many porches have been reincarnated as permanent rooms because they can be easily converted. The key, however, is knowing when to reinvent a porch as part of the house and when to leave it as it was intended. Most porches on older homes were built to lighter specifica-tions than the structure they are attached to. While you can modify them to meet current building codes, you have to weigh the additional expense against the payback for that investment.

Just because a porch can be converted into permanent living space doesn't mean it should be. There's many a "remuddling" of charming old Victorian houses where the owner enclosed the front porch. Yes, it adds warm living space to the front of the house, but it destroys the value of the architecture and consequently the value of the house.

However, the side and back porches of a Dutch Colonial or farm-house are good candidates for conversion to living space. Often the porches were built on the side or rear of the house, usually with entry from the kitchen. The porch had three exterior walls with large screen windows and walls trimmed in bead board as wainscoting. The wall between the interior and porch was often finished with the exterior sid-ing. The porch was covered by the roof, which extended over and enclosed it.

Conversion Possibilities

The location of the porch is the first thing that determines its potential use. For example, the floor plan for a kitchen will be enhanced with an adjacent back porch because it provides expansion space for an eat-in kitchen or kitchen and family room. A side porch off a living or dining room makes a convenient location for a den or library or playroom. Converting a porch usually involves insulating the walls and ceiling, adding or upgrading the windows, adding heat and electricity, and finishing the interior with wallboard, flooring, and woodwork.

Investigating a Porch Down Under

Before you make any decision about converting a porch to year-round living space, do some investigation work to appraise its construction and condition. Get a flashlight, measuring tape, and a clipboard with notepad and poke around underneath the porch to see what's down there. If you have knee pads, wear them. Make a sketch and take measurements of the length and width of the four sides and the height of the walls to see how high it is off the ground.

Floor Joists and Beams

Look at the size and direction of the floor joists and the spans of the main beams, which bear the full load of the floor joists. Code specifications will vary according to the size of the porch, but two-by-six floor joists on 16-inch centers should be considered minimum requirements.

Footings

Inspect the footings and posts in the corners and along the sides that support the porch. Brick piers should have all mortar joints filled and show no signs of cracking.

Pest Damage

In the framing beneath the porch, look for signs of wood rot or damage from termites, carpenter ants, or beetles, any of which could require more extensive repair and replacement work.

Lines, Ducts, and Pipes

Find the electrical lines, heating ducts, and plumbing pipes, and see how they are routed under or near the porch. If these utilities are near the porch, it is easier and less expensive to tap into them. This is especially true if you want to tie into an existing forced-air heating/cooling system. Long duct runs are expensive to install, and they reduce the efficiency of the system.

Also inspect the basement or crawl space adjacent to the porch and note the location of these utilities before completing plans.

If after giving the porch a going-over you find that there are many problems and the porch needs repair, use this information as a bargaining chip when negotiating the price. The costs of extensive repairs are difficult to fully recover. For the property to be marketable it must be in good repair. Have the cost of needed repairs reflect a reduced purchase price; don't expect the repairs to greatly increase the value of the property.

Evaluating the Porch Interior

Measuring and appraising the interior is easier than crawling around on your hands and knees. Make a rough sketch of the interior noting the length and width of the walls, the size of the windows, and the height of the ceiling.

If the porch will be a stand-alone room with the same entrance, like a den off of a dining room, the conversion issues are straightforward. However, it becomes a major project if the porch will become part of another room, like an eat-in kitchen, which involves converting the space and making the transition to the existing house appear as if it's part of the house and not an appendage to it. On the outside the exterior siding on the porch should be aesthetically pleasing and match or blend with the existing siding. Windows, doors, and trim should be the same style as the house so that from outward appearance the porch is part of the house.

Inside, the attention to detail makes the difference between a new space appearing tacked on or being an integral part of the house. The transition can be achieved by using the same flooring material in the new space and duplicating the woodwork and trim from the existing house throughout the porch conversion.

Climate Control

Talk to an HVAC contractor about heating and air-conditioning a porch conversion. The pro will inspect the existing heating and cooling unit to see if it can be tapped into or if an auxiliary unit is needed. Many older houses we remodeled had a furnace or boiler with the extra capacity to heat an enclosed porch because the unit was oversized to begin with. And it had even greater capacity after we upgraded the energy efficiency of the house by adding insulation and weather stripping. This may not be true for newer houses, which have furnaces with capacities carefully matched to the size of the house. In such cases a heating contractor can advise you.

Windows and Siding

Most porch windows are old and uninsulated so replacing them is necessary. Look at the style and size of windows throughout the house and choose new ones to match. Use siding that matches or blends with the existing siding to enhance the exterior.

Ceiling and Walls

Many porch ceilings and walls are clad in bead board and not insulated. In some, the interior wall is actually the exterior siding. Insulating the ceiling and three exterior walls will dramatically improve space; framing, drywall, and woodwork will make it a room.

LESSONS LEARNED

We found that baseboard-radiant electric heat is probably the easiest heating system to install in a porch, although it is expensive to operate. But we couldn't use it every time we wanted to. Unlike furnaces, existing electrical panels seldom have excess capacity. One house had an electrical panel with only 100-amp capacity, which allowed us to add a branch circuit for lighting and receptacles but not for radiant electric heat (that usually requires 150 amps). We installed baseboard hot-water heat instead, tapping into the existing hydronic system.

Floors

To create a natural transition from a porch to the house, we raise the porch floor level (if necessary) by building it up with sleepers and plywood sheeting. Then we finish the floor to match the adjoining room's floor (usually carpeting or hardwood) and use a low-level door threshold. We remove the door to the porch and its trim around the doorjamb, which widens the opening, then finish the space with wallboard.

Use the worksheet in Figure 13.3 when inspecting a porch to take notes and review when you're making a decision about whether to expand it.

Figure 13.3 Porch Worksheet

NOTES

Access to porch

Adjoining what room? _____

Width of door _____

Floor Plan of Interior Space

Length, width, and height _____

Walls and Ceiling

Cladding _____

Condition _____

Insulation _____

Windows

Sizes to remove _____

Sizes to replace _____

Flooring

Material   _____

Condition   _____

Utilities

Electrical receptacles   _____

Light fixture   _____

Heating/cooling   _____

Foundation

Length, width, and depth   _____

Floor Joists and Beams

Size and material   _____

Condition   _____

Covered with insulation   _____

Footings

Location and number   _____

Condition   _____

Utilities

Electrical lines   _____

Heating ducts   _____

Plumbing pipes   _____

Ground

Condition of soil   _____

CHAPTER 14

WHO DOES THE WORK? WHO MANAGES THE JOB?

The answers to the two questions about who does the work and who manages the job shouldn't be taken lightly because the answers are important to the success of a rehab project whether you resell, rent, or live in the property. The duration of work and what it costs is the key to a quick turnaround if you're investing to resell the property. The under-construction time may be even more important if the renovation is extensive and you're living in the house while it is being remodeled.

There are many work and management scenarios investors devise, but for your first investment property, we caution you to be conservative in your estimates of time, projected costs, and skill level. In other words, don't quit your day job, buy a fixer-upper, and dive into the project without fully understanding the management skills and construction expertise that are needed.

Being physically fit isn't a prerequisite for rehabbing, but being in shape sure helps if you plan to do some or all of the work. You'll quickly learn that slinging a hammer and hanging wallboard are not jobs for the faint of heart. Hauling heavy materials, working on your hands and knees driving screws in a deck, and crouching underneath a sink fixing a leak are demanding physical jobs and require a lot more stamina than does working at a desk. Rehabbing gives you a good workout, not to mention a few aches and pains.

Multitasking: Wearing Many Hats on the Job

Planning the work schedule of a rehab property requires a different set of management skills from those needed in an office job. Granted, there are very few interoffice memos to digest and even fewer meaningless meetings to attend. But there are many high-level skills needed—making on-the-spot decisions, scheduling the work of subcontractors who have many other clients besides you, ordering the correct amount of materials, coping with work delays and interruptions because of weather, and dealing with building inspectors. The stress and hassles of business travel may soon be replaced by waiting for a plumber to arrive to complete a job before a scheduled inspection or rescheduling work because of a freak hailstorm. Giving a PowerPoint presentation might seem like a walk in the park compared with some of the day-to-day adjustments required in your house rehab.

Do All or Some or None of the Work

Your first decision is whether you should do all the rehab work from start to finish, or do some of the subcontracting work, or act as the general contractor and manage the project, or hire a general contractor to manage the project. Let's look at each of these possibilities.

You Do All the Work

If you're retired and have time on your side, you are in an ideal situation to do all the work yourself and putz around the property working at your own speed and enjoying the process. If you have a day job, don't quit it until you've first bought and sold a property on a part-time basis. Rehabbing a house for rent or resale is a full time, short-term job that ends only when the property is sold or rented and the profit is in your pocket.

Hire Yourself as a Subcontractor

Another twist to this scenario is if you do some of the work and act as a subcontractor who will complete some phase or phases of the work so you don't have to pay someone to do it. For example, the initial grunt work of removing old kitchen cabinets, flooring, or wallpaper is ideally suited for a handy property owner. You can pay the tradespeople to do installations and get in and get out without charging you for the tear-out work.

But be realistic about your time and talents. It will cost you money if you take on a phase of the work and then don't complete it. There's nothing worse than a no-show property owner who keeps hired workers from completing their jobs and consequently delays the work flow.

Another advantage of hiring yourself as a subcontractor is obvious—the savings in labor costs will flow to the bottom line. There's an additional benefit if the improvement funds come from a bank loan that includes labor costs. By paying yourself for the labor you can create a cash flow during the rehab phase of the property. It doesn't matter who does the work to make improvements that add value to the property.

You Act as a General Contractor and Hire Subs

If you're good at multitasking and can keep your day job to support you, consider acting as the general contractor. This role requires free time during the day every week, so if you work nights and are available during the day, it's an option to consider. During the day you have to manage the job—make phone calls, check on the delivery of materials, find out if workers showed up, or schedule an appointment with a plumber or building inspector. Being the general contractor, you're responsible for managing and controlling the project, but you aren't required to do the actual work.

The challenge is managing the work of others while you're not on-site 24 hours a day, seven days a week. Of course, cell phones have made this job easier, but it still requires management skills like scheduling different jobs so they mesh and don't overlap and confronting workers who don't show up—or do show up, but don't perform work that meets your expectations. If you can finesse the time during your day job and are good at making follow-up calls, working out contingency plans, and thinking on your feet, you'll make a good general contractor.

Here's where having a partnership with another investor works very well in rehabbing a house. Or if you're working and living in a rehab house, if one partner is a stay-at-home worker, "being there" is a key advantage.

Hire a General Contractor to Oversee the Project

Typically a general contractor charges 15 to 25 percent of the total cost of a project, so right off the bat, you have to add that expense to the cost of the job. However, if you or a partner is not able to be there and manage the progress, it's money well spent because the longer a property lingers without improvements being made, the more money is eaten up on the loan side.

Keeping Records, Staying in Touch

Whether you're doing the work, managing others, or hiring a general contractor to manage the property rehab, it's important for you to keep records—of everything.

- **Material samples and product information.** Use a box, canvas sack, or briefcase to keep product samples and brochures.
- **Price quotes, bid sheets.** Keep estimates for work and correspondence with suppliers and contractors in a pocket notebook.
- **Contact information.** Stay in touch with workers by having a readily available list of phone numbers and e-mail addresses. Keep the list on paper, a laptop, or a PDA (personal digital assistant).
- **Log sheet of phone calls.** It doesn't have to be detailed, just keep a record of the date and subject of your conversations with workers, suppliers, and brokers. It's a good way to keep track of your communications.

Checklist for Managing a Home Rehab

If you are willing to admit you're fallible, you'll agree that it's more than handy to have a reference for all the details involved in rehabbing a house, especially if you're managing the project. Even if you've hired a general contractor to make things happen, you should have a handle on the project and know how the work is progressing. The checklist we use is nothing more than a laundry list of the work required to bring a house to market. However you're involved in the work, adapt the checklist to your needs. Whether you use paper and a clipboard, a laptop, or a personal digital assistant, use the checklist in Figure 14.1 or make your own as a reference.

Finding a Good Contractor and Subcontractors

Have you ever been at a cocktail party where the hot topic of discussion is not politics or sports or movies—it's contractors? We've heard countless stories from friends, relatives, and total strangers about their experiences dealing with no-show contractors or their praise and admiration for the precision work of their tile installers. When you find a good contractor who is a joy to work with, rehabbing can be enjoyable. Our experience has been that we treat them well and they usually do the same to us.

Many contractors prefer working with investors instead of home owners because investors know what they want done, they don't change their mind, and they can lead to more work and become steady customers when they continue to invest and rehab property on a regular basis. These traits are appealing to a specialty contractor who wants to get in and out of a job without a lot of hassles.

To develop a list of reliable contractors and specialty subcontractors takes time, but with each job you'll find those you like to work with. For a first-time investor looking for a contractor, there are two basic approaches. In the first, you do the search and find the contractor; in the second, you use a service to find the contractor.

You Do the Search

The best reference for a contractor that you can get comes from someone you know. Maybe it's another investor or a friend or a real estate

Figure 14.1 Checklist for Managing a Home Rehab

	WORK DESCRIPTION	COMPLETED
Exterior Siding		
Condition	_____	
Other issues	_____	
Foundation		
Support columns or piers	_____	
Exterior Plumbing		
Spigot(s)	_____	
Meter	_____	
Electrical Service		
Meter	_____	
Wires and cables	_____	
Crawl Space		
Condition of support posts, bolts	_____	
Other issues	_____	
Deck or Patio		
Condition of material, railings	_____	
Other issues	_____	
Roof and Chimney		
Condition	_____	
Flashing	_____	
Gutters, downspouts, diverters	_____	
Other issues	_____	

Sidewalk and Driveway

Condition of surface, grading,
   low areas

   _____

Other issues

   _____

Doors and Storm Doors

Condition

   _____

Lock

   _____

Storm screen and glass panel

   _____

Door threshold

   _____

Other issues

   _____

Windows and Storms

Condition

   _____

Glass

   _____

Caulking

   _____

Storm screen and glass panel

   _____

Other issues

   _____

Heating/Cooling Unit

Condition

   _____

Other issues

   _____

Garage, Outbuildings

Siding

   _____

Foundation and grading

   _____

Doors and windows

   _____

Roof, gutters, downspouts

   _____

Interior floor and walls

   _____

Electrical power   _____

Other issues   _____

Landscaping and Trees

Lawn   _____

Garden beds   _____

Trees and shrubbery   _____

Other issues   _____

Living/Dining Room

Walls and ceiling   _____

Doors   _____

Windows   _____

Floor   _____

Fireplace   _____

Built-ins   _____

Electrical outlets   _____

Lighting   _____

HVAC   _____

Other issues   _____

Kitchen

Walls and ceiling   _____

Doors   _____

Windows   _____

Floor   _____

Appliances: stove, oven, range, vent,
    refrigerator, disposal, dishwasher   _____

Sink and faucet   _____

Cabinets and countertops   _____

Electrical system   _____

GFCI outlets: adequate number and
    placement   _____

Lighting   _____

HVAC   _____

Other issues   _____

Electrical Service Panel

Bathroom 1

Walls and ceiling   _____

Doors   _____

Windows   _____

Floor   _____

Toilet   _____

Sink, faucet, cabinet   _____

Storage   _____

Accessories   _____

GFCI outlets: adequate number and
    placement   _____

Lighting   _____

HVAC   _____

Other issues   _____

Bathroom 2

Walls and ceiling   _____

Doors   _____

Windows   _____

Floor   _____

Toilet   _____

Sink, faucet, cabinet   _____

Storage   _____

Accessories   _____

GFCI outlets: adequate number
   and placement   _____

Lighting   _____

HVAC   _____

Other issues   _____

Bedroom 1

Walls and ceiling   _____

Doors   _____

Windows   _____

Floor   _____

Closet   _____

Electrical   _____

Lighting   _____

HVAC   _____

Other issues   _____

Bedroom 2

Walls and ceiling   _____

Doors   _____

Windows   _____

Floor   _____

Closet   _____

Electrical _____

Lighting _____

HVAC _____

Other issues _____

Bedroom 3

Walls and ceiling _____

Doors _____

Windows _____

Floor _____

Closet _____

Electrical _____

Lighting _____

HVAC _____

Other issues _____

Family Room

Walls and ceiling _____

Doors _____

Windows _____

Floor _____

Fireplace _____

Built-ins _____

Electrical _____

Lighting _____

HVAC _____

Other issues _____

Halls and Closets

Walls and ceiling _____

Doors _____

Windows _____

Floor _____

Stairs _____

Smoke/CO detectors _____

Other issues _____

Attic

Finished, unfinished _____

Rafters _____

Ventilation _____

Insulation _____

Stairs and access _____

Other issues _____

Basement

Unfinished _____

Partially finished _____

Humidity, odors, water seepage _____

Walls and ceiling _____

Doors _____

Windows _____

Floor _____

Lighting and electrical _____

Plumbing pipes, water meter _____

Stairs: balusters on steps, handrail
   on wall   _____

Other   _____

Laundry and appliances   _____

Dryer: secure hose connection; vent
   to outside, grounded   _____

Washer: braided stainless steel
   pressurized washer hoses,
   grounded   _____

Other issues   _____

Sump Pump and Floor Drain

Furnace or Heat Pump

Secure ductwork, clean filter   _____

Other issues   _____

Hot-Water Heater

Gas or electric, adequate capacity   _____

Other issues   _____

broker. The best choice is someone who has had work completed by a contractor whom he or she would hire again. If you can take a look at the work before calling the contractor, that's even better.

If you can't get a referral from a friend who recommends a contractor, look to a local building-supply dealer; often they will recommend a contractor who is one of their customers. The last alternative is to make cold calls to contractors listed in the Yellow Pages or advertised in a local newspaper.

Home-Center-Installed Sales and Design Services

Using the installation service from the retailer where you buy materials is another way to find a contractor. Most of the major retailers and building-supply centers offer an "installed sale" price on their merchandise. This includes big-ticket items such as roofing, siding, replacement windows, and heating and cooling systems as well as the most popular installed materials like flooring, doors, window treatments, water heaters, and all built-in appliances.

This is a turnkey service that's popular with consumers who don't have the time to find or can't find references. It's also a solution for a property investor because it eliminates the process of finding contractors. In most of these agreements the retailers imply they stand behind the installation, which is something to ask about. The agreement should clarify the responsibilities of the customer, the contractor, and the retailer.

If the kitchen or bathroom needs more than a cosmetic face-lift, the design service at home centers is a great help. Make an appointment with a design specialist, bring accurate measurements (snapshots are helpful, too) of a kitchen or bathroom, and you can work with the specialist to choose materials and lay out the design of the room. Be up-front about your budget and the specialist will direct you to a design using cabinets and appliances to fit and will manage the installation. Sometimes there's a design fee in the $100 range that is applied to the purchase of the materials. The service saves you a tremendous amount of time and anguish in maximizing your investment in these two important rooms.

Using an Online Contractor's Referral Service

Who would have thought you could use the worldwide Internet to find a contractor in your neighborhood? Online referral businesses like servicemagic.com and improvenet.com are lead-generation services or networks that offer an alternative way to find a good contractor because they connect qualified customers with qualified contractors—a win-win situation for both parties. When contractors join and become a member of the network, they are prescreened and profiled by the service ensuring they have a clean legal and credit history, current insurance, and a license to practice. They pay for leads to new customers, typically anywhere from $10 for a plumbing repair to $50 for a bathroom remodeling project. Sometimes the contractor pays more if the lead turns into a sale. Some of these services are free for home owners; others require an annual membership fee.

At their websites you'll be asked to enter a detailed description of the project so the members of the network in your area can decide if they'd like to bid on the job. Your project description is e-mailed to the specialty contractor members who serve your location. Based on that and their availability, they respond to the service and then are referred to you.

First Impressions

If you use a retailer-installed sales service or an online referral service, a contractor will call you. If you do the search, you'll make the initial phone call to a short list of contractors and subcontractors you want to consider. Use your notebook to keep a record of who and when you call. Make sure you have a succinct message so when you're prompted to leave an answering machine message you can quickly explain your interest in calling. Tell them your phone number and the best time for you to receive calls. Explain your time frame and that your project is an investment property.

When you speak with contractors, find out if they are licensed and insured for workers' compensation, property damage, and personal liability. Ask a lot of questions: Do they like working on investment property? Typically how many projects do they have going on at the same time? Do they work alone or have helpers? Ask about their availability.

Be able to clearly describe the project. For example, if you're talking to a painting contractor you should know the approximate room sizes and condition of the walls. A flooring installer will want to know the room size and how many layers of material are already on the floor. A roofer will ask if the roof is leaking and if there are multiple layers of shingles. Certainly you can't be expected to know everything before talking with a contractor, but you should know the basics of the work that's required.

Ask the contractor for names of satisfied customers and call them. When you do, ask if you can see the contractor's work at their home.

Usually people are willing to let you take a look, especially if they liked the contractor and think their cooperation will bring the contractor more work.

LESSONS LEARNED

We found the best time to reach most contractors is first thing in the morning. They're usually on the road early with a cell phone in their ear so they're available to talk with or leave a voice message.

Staying in Touch Is a Top Priority

If you're managing the job and working at the property or have a partner who is, staying in touch with contractors is easy. You're right there and available to make a decision or adjust your schedule if necessary. The challenge is keeping that line of communication open when you're at the office—or worse, out of town—and the workers are at the job site. Of course, cell phones have changed the way all of us communicate, but playing telephone tag can be frustrating for a contractor and investor, so we see a tremendous advantage in being on-site or having a partner who is.

To keep things on track, establish a weekly update meeting or walkthrough. Friday is a good day to do a lot of things: review the progress of the week, make sure the next week's materials are on-site, and discuss any upcoming issues. You can ask what the workers are scheduled to complete the next week and if any materials or deliveries are expected. Being on-site is the best way to keep track, but if that's not possible a weekly scheduled update can be made by phone or e-mail. The point is that as the property owner, you need to know that the various workers are coordinated so the work flow continues without stopping.

Punch List

A punch list is a contractor's to-do list of everything that is not completed or anything that requires fixing or replacement. As a property owner, you should keep a close eye on the progress of work and keep your own punch list of things needing repair or correction. Use the list so that when you communicate regularly with the contractor, you can point out the items and look for others. Figure 14.2 is a sample contractor's punch list.

A Good Contract: Putting It in Writing

The Remodelers Council of the National Association of Home Builders suggests what should be in a remodeling agreement. As a legal document, the contract between you and a contractor should spell out the what, where, how, time span, and cost of your project. It should be clear, complete, and concise and include the provisions that follow. When a contractor presents a contract to you to authorize work, make sure you understand the details before signing it.

The Main Agreement

- Name the property owner and the contractor and their state or local jurisdiction license or registration number.
- List the address or legal description of the property found on the deed.
- Give a detailed description of the project.
- List all work to be done, including the specifications for the work and the contractor's warranty. To avoid confusion, this may specify work that will *not* be done or that someone else will do.
- Include a visual representation, such as a floor plan, blueprint, or sketch that illustrates what the contractor will do and where.
- Specify a project time table that includes estimated start and completion dates. This may include language that stipulates

Figure 14.2 Punch List

Property owner _____

Property address _____

Contact information _____

General or subcontractor _____

Contact information _____

Punch List Items	**Date**	**Approved by**
_____		
_____		
_____		
_____		
_____		
_____		
_____		
_____		
_____		
_____		
_____		
_____		
_____		
_____		
_____		

Completed punch list items submitted by _____

Contractor _____

All items accepted as completed by _____

Owner _____

conditions about adverse weather that would require an extension of the completion date.

- Price and payment schedule should indicate how much you must pay at the start of and at specified intervals during the project and at completion. The agreement should mention any deposits you may have already made.
- A predetermined bonus for early completion is sometimes included to provide an incentive for a contractor to finish the work ahead of schedule.
- Sometimes a liquidated damages clause is included that requires payment of a predetermined amount of money for breach of contract, such as an unreasonably late completion of the project or failure to pay subcontractors or material supplier and present necessary lien waivers.
- A section may stipulate a date by which you must sign the contract to obtain the price quoted.

All parties to the agreement must sign it. Each of you should retain a signed original for your records. When the agreement is signed, both you and the contractor should initial and receive a complete set of drawings, plans, and specifications.

General Conditions of a Contract

- The contract should include a section about who will obtain and pay for any necessary building permits and other approvals. It may also specify that the contractor agrees to comply with all applicable health and building codes, statutes, regulations, and ordinances governing the work and the way the contractor performs it.
- The contract usually lists the insurance the project requires, including the contractor's policies that cover employees, subcontractors, and the project, such as workers' compensation and liability insurance. It may also list any increase in home owner's insurance you will need to carry.

- A section should explain the possibility of unforeseeable conditions (such as rusty pipes behind a wall or under a floor) and provide a contingency in case these conditions increase the price of the job.
- The contract gives procedures to follow if hazardous materials—such as lead paint, radon, or asbestos—are encountered on the job site. You may agree in advance that you will hire specialty abatement contractors to remove the materials. This allows the contractor to suspend activity on the project until the appropriate specialty contractor takes care of the hazard.
- The people who work on or provide materials for a project are legally entitled to obtain a specific interest in or to place a lien on the property if you do not pay them. The contract should require that you receive a lien release (either partial or final depending upon the type of payment) when you make payments to the contractor. By signing a lien release, your contractor and suppliers waive their rights to place a lien on your property.
- A contract should include a list of anyone other than the contractor and crew who will work on your house. Even if it is you, the owner, it should be spelled out in the contract assuring that the contractor is not responsible for that work and that he or she will not guarantee it.
- A change order is a written agreement to alter the work described in the original contract. It details how you can make changes after work has begun and protects the contractor from dealing with a series of revisions that could greatly alter the cost and completion of the project. If there is payment required for a change order, it is stipulated. Figure 14.3 is a sample change order.

Working Conditions

A description of the working conditions and how the workers can affect the conditions may be handled in a separate form or during a preconstruction meeting rather than included in the original agreement.

- **Access and working hours.** Your contract may indicate how workers can access the work site; restrict access to the work area

Figure 14.3 Change Order

Date: _____

Original date of contract: _____

Property address: _____

Property owner: _____

Contractor: _____

Change order number: _____

Request for Change Order

The undersigned owner and contractor agree to approve and perform work that is substantially different from the original scope of the project. Both parties know that the requested changes, which are listed below, may change the price and completion schedule. Any differences in the cost of the project relating to this change order will be taken into account for the regular payment schedule.

The contractor will perform the following work:

_____

_____

_____

_____

_____

_____

_____

The total cost for labor and materials to be added or deducted: _____

How the change will affect the completion schedule: _____

New estimated completion date: _____

Contractor approval and date: _____
                              Signature

Owner approval and date: _____
                        Signature

by children, pets, and other unauthorized persons; and specify the
working hours workers may be on the premises.

- **Care of the premises.** Any specific steps you and the crew will
  take to preserve landscaping and protect rooms not being
  remodeled are specified.
- **Bathroom and phone.** Whether workers may have the use of
  your property's bathroom and telephone is specified; otherwise,
  the location for a portable toilet is decided.
- **Smoking, radios.** If workers are prohibited from smoking on the
  premises or playing a loud radio, that information will appear in
  the contract.
- **Cleanup and trash removal.** The responsibilities, schedules, and
  procedures for daily and final cleanup are specified, as is the extent
  of daily "broom clean" cleanup; also, conditions of the property
  when the job is completed should include specific information such
  as "Dumpster removed," "all debris removed," and so on.
- **Personal property.** If someone is responsible for removing the
  property owner's tools or materials, it should be specified. And if
  items are to be saved from demolition, it should be noted where
  they should be stored.
- **Sign posting.** If a contractor wants to post his or her sign, that
  should be included in the contract along with the size of the sign
  and the length of time it will be on the property.
- **Rescission right.** By law, all home-improvement contracts are
  required to give you three days to change your mind and cancel
  after signing.
- **Dispute resolution.** A clause should detail the terms of dispute
  resolution and arbitration procedures as a way to resolve a
  problem if it arises.

Warranty

If the contractor offers a warranty, the description may appear in the
contract or as a separate document referenced in the contract. The warranty will explain the responsibilities of the contractor regarding workmanship and materials. This document typically provides a limited

guarantee that, if the work on the project does not meet accepted industry practices, the contractor will make repairs or replacements or provide a refund as necessary. Many contractors will guarantee their workmanship for one year.

Checklist Before Signing a Contract

After reading a contract and asking any questions you have, read the document again. Does it include these items?

- Name, address, and business phone number of the contractor
- Start and finish date
- Method, amount, and payment schedule
- Detailed written specifications of design and products
- A system to handle changes
- A description of your lien rights, dispute resolution, and the contractor's warranty
- A statement of a right to change your mind and cancel the contract within 72 hours

Timing and Money Disbursement

Contractors have their own policies about down payments and their preferred payment schedules. Many work on a three-part payment schedule that works like this: you pay one-third of the total price when signing the contract (down payment), another third when the work is half completed, and the final third when all the building inspections have been successfully completed and the house is ready to occupy. Often 10 percent of the total amount is held back as an incentive to the contractor for completing any last-minute work. In some arrangements the same scheduling is used but on a quarterly basis.

If you're financing your project with a loan, make sure the loan-disbursement schedule is in sync with your contractor's billing intervals. For example, if the payment schedule for the contractor is February 1, the loan disbursement should have been received by the last week of January so there is time for money to be deposited and checks issued.

Time and Material for Services

Some subcontractors doing a specific job want to be paid on a time and material basis, also called cost-plus. For example, a mason repairing a chimney might say he can't accurately bid the job because he has to do some investigating before getting under way. In that instance, he'll charge an hourly rate plus the cost of the new materials needed. We haven't been burned using this arrangement, but it makes it very difficult to calculate your expenses with unknown costs.

CHAPTER 15

SELLING FOR A PROFIT

The seller's responsibilities begin with getting the property ready for the market and end with handing over the keys to the house at the property settlement. By the time a rehabbed house is ready for market, the work has been completed and should make any broker pleased to show it. The first part of this chapter suggests additional steps to make the house as appealing as it can be. The rest of the chapter explains what's involved in the house-selling process, whether using a listing agent or selling "by owner."

On the Home Front

A recently renovated house without furniture has a distinct advantage over a house full of furniture because the empty rooms make the property look more spacious. Buyers can imagine their furniture more easily when there's fresh paint on the walls, a clean floor, and no signs of everyday things like toys and newspapers that give a house a lived-in look.

Before posting the For Sale sign in the yard and allowing the house to be shown to anyone, take time for a final push to assure that the house is clean and inviting. The goal is to create maximum curb appeal so that the first impression a buyer has when he or she pulls up in front of the house is positive. Inside, make the rooms look attractive and uncluttered so the buyer is excited and wants to make the house his or her own.

Curb Appeal

Experienced real estate agents tell us that the initial impression prospective buyers form as they first see a property is very important. It's called "curb appeal." These same agents say it is difficult to get buyers to even get out of the car if they don't like what they see. So what makes a property have good curb appeal? That's not an easy question to answer because each buyer has individual tastes and expectations, but we can tell you that anything that hints of neglect is a turnoff.

The buyers' first impression is an overall wide-screen view of the property, so if it is favorable they will probably want to take a closer look. Here are some low- or no-cost chores to make a positive first impression on a prospective buyer. Time and money spent improving the curb appeal will provide some of the highest returns of any improvement you can make.

Squeaky-Clean and Inviting

These tidy-up chores and last-minute additions go a long way toward showing the house in its best light and indicating a pride of ownership that influences a prospective buyer. Remember, the house may have been a construction site for a while and you are used to walking past piles of rubble, but the buyer is not.

Landscaping

For the duration that the house is on the market and under contract, keep the lawn and garden trimmed and manicured. Make sure the lawn is mowed regularly, the garden beds are edged, and the trees and shrubbery are trimmed.

Front Door

To make the front entrance inviting, lay down a new doormat and hang a wreath on the door. If weather permits, add a container of colorful flowers next to the door or on the porch, and keep them watered.

Garbage

Be vigilant about removing all garbage, debris, and scrap materials. Haul away or have removed anything that's old and unusable. Double-check that no construction debris is left lying around. Rake the ground around the building to gather up paint chips and any old materials.

Light Fixtures

Go through the house and put new lightbulbs in the fixtures. If a room does not have a ceiling fixture, put a floor lamp in the room so anyone touring the house at night will be able to see it. Put the lamp near the door so if the house is shown in the evening, the broker can turn on the light easily. Change any lightbulbs in exterior lights, especially lights at the front and back doors and garage.

Floors

Throughout the house, wash all floors and clean and vacuum carpeting. Remove floor heating registers and vacuum inside them. Protect the clean floors at the front and back doors with a clean drop cloth or rug.

Closets

Remove hangers and clean out the shelves and floor of all closets. Check that the closet lights work.

Windows

Wash all the windows, including patio sliding doors.

Kitchen

Thoroughly clean all appliances, countertops, and kitchen cabinets, inside and out. If needed, add new shelf paper to line cabinet shelves.

Bathroom

Thoroughly clean all the fixtures including toilet, bathtub, and vanity cabinet. If you haven't already done so, make sure the tile grout is clean. Remove any mineral deposits on the showerhead.

Laundry Room

Thoroughly clean the washer and dryer, and remove any debris that was left in the area.

Attic, Basement, and Garage

If you have not painted the basement, use a shop vacuum to remove dust, dirt, and spiderwebs in rafters and on the walls and floor. Remove any debris or materials that were left by the previous owner. Straighten and organize storm windows and other stored items that remain with the house. Check that the light fixtures are in working order.

If You Are Living in the House

Declutter everywhere, removing stacks of newspapers and magazines and stuff inside closets and cabinets. Use three boxes for stuff you remove: one box to toss, sell, or donate; another to keep; and one for stuff in limbo that you can't decide about.

Don't have a television in the living room. It adds to the clutter and tips buyers off that the house is so small this is the only place for the TV. Remove the coffee maker, can opener, and other appliances in the kitchen to free up countertop space. Remove a third of the furnishings in every room to make them appear more spacious. Organize and clean bookcases and shelves throughout the house.

Secrets from House Stagers

A stager is a designer or someone with design experience who helps a home owner market his or her house to its full potential. They usually work with sellers of high-end properties on a consulting basis. The stager surveys the property and makes specific recommendations. Frequently stagers are brought in by the listing real estate broker to suggest changes that edit out the extraneous items that have meaning for the owners but do nothing to make the house appealing to a buyer. To put it bluntly, they usually recommend getting rid of most of that precious personal stuff filling up many homes.

They start with the obvious—clean the house thoroughly, make it smell fresh, and clean and get rid of stuff to make a house appear larger. Stagers know time-stretched buyers want a turnkey house, one that's ready to move into and doesn't require remodeling. Stagers routinely suggest painting the walls and ceilings and replacing old carpeting. They often suggest replacing clashing or outdated wallpaper with a basic paint job. Once decorating is completed, they rearrange the pared-down furnishings and sometimes bring in their own accessories to add props to the house.

On the Sales Front

The house-selling process is the same as when you are a buyer; however, your perspective as the seller of investment property is different. If you use a real estate broker to list the property, the listing agent takes on the responsibility of advertising, showing the house, and representing your interest when a buyer makes an offer to purchase the house. If you sell the property "by owner" those responsibilities fall to you. Of course, selling a house yourself puts more money in your pocket because you don't have to pay a commission.

Discover Potential Problems Presale

The most important point to remember is that the same tactics that buyers use to get a good deal can be used against you as the seller. Any problem with the property that a home inspector may turn up can cost you more to negotiate during the sale than it would to fix beforehand.

It is money well spent to hire a home inspector to do a presale inspection. Most home inspectors will charge considerably less for a presale inspection if you do not require an extensive report. There's more about hiring a home inspector in Chapter 10, "Buying the Property."

A presale inspection will help you identify any problems that could prevent or delay the sale of the house. There's nothing worse than getting a nice offer, accepting it, and then having a home inspection turn up a serious termite problem. It is better to take care of these conditions before the house is on the market.

If any problems are detected, discuss them with the inspector, an attorney, or your real estate broker. Most state real estate sales laws make it your responsibility as seller to disclose information about defects of the property that could influence someone's decision to buy the house. They include structural defects and health risks such as lead, asbestos, radon, formaldehyde, and carbon monoxide.

Listing with a Real Estate Broker

A listing agreement is a contract that spells out the legal relationship between a seller and a real estate brokerage firm. It states that the property owner gives the real estate company a specified amount of time to sell the property and receive a commission or a percentage of the sales price. Some sellers retain the right to sell the property themselves (and not pay a commission), but this doesn't hold much appeal to a real estate company that is going to spend time and money advertising and showing the property.

A listing agreement is a written contract that includes the following items:

- The name and location of the property and owner
- The listing real estate broker and company
- Sales price
- Commission
- Type of listing
- Length of contract (expiration date)
- Signatures
- Termination clause if either party wants to cancel the contract
- Items included in the sale of the property, e.g., appliances, window treatments, carpeting
- Offers and how and when they are presented
- Deposit of earnest money
- Broker responsibilities

When a seller signs a listing agreement with a broker it's a partnership with one goal in mind: finding a buyer for the property and closing the deal. The job of the property owner is to hand over the keys to a house that is clean and appealing and then get out of the way and let the professionals show the house to prospective buyers. The listing broker submits the listing to the listing service he or she subscribes to, which then gives the information to a network of real estate brokers. One day a week on a regular basis there is an open house for real estate agents to tour recently listed property. These agents have client rosters of buyers looking for specific types of houses in specific neighborhoods, so there is often a flurry of showings after the agents see a new listing and make appointments with prospective clients.

Evaluating an Offer to Purchase

There are three basic things to consider when a broker presents the seller with an offer: the price, the financial terms, and the closing date. If there is more than one offer, the listing broker should present them all at the same time for comparison. Because investment property is ready for occupancy, closing sooner rather than later is the priority. The best offer may not always be the one with the highest price. Take into consideration how qualified the buyer is. A fast closing date will save you money and get you your cash quicker. Look at the sale in total, not just price.

Making a Counteroffer

Unless you are selling the property yourself, the actual negotiating over the price and terms of the contract is the job of the real estate broker; that's what you're paying him or her for. If the offer does not meet your expectations, talk it over with the broker and instruct him or her to make a counteroffer.

Use the Seller's Checklist in Figure 15.1 to guide you through the responsibilities and process of selling your house.

Figure 15.1 Seller's Checklist

Before you sign a contract to list your property for sale, take the time to make it as desirable and market-ready as you can. Use this checklist to guide you through the sales process.

TASKS	DATE	NOTES
Order a presale inspection of the property		
Review the terms of the listing contract		
Complete all improvement projects		
Complete all cleaning tasks		
Remove all garbage, debris, and materials		
Check that home insurance coverage includes the house being on the market		
Order extra set of keys for broker		
Consult with utility companies about changing names on service records		
Schedule final walk-through		
Review final settlement statement		
Arrange to make loan payoff with lender		
Stop service on all utilities		
Discontinue insurance		
Get address of settlement location		
Make loan payoff to lender		

For Sale by Owner (FSBO)

We think there are far more disadvantages than advantages to selling by owner. An owner-seller can't compete with the hundreds of brokers who in turn have qualified buyers who are interested in buying a house—possibly the one you have for sale. Maybe if after rehabbing and selling several investment properties you want to tackle the job, it's worth considering. But for the first-time investor, definitely plan to pay a broker to list and sell your property.

You're more likely to be successful at selling an investment property yourself if the market is very active, with more buyers than sellers. You also must have a flexible schedule that allows you to show the property at any time. You must be available to meet prospective buyers at their convenience, which can be day or night or on weekends.

A sales background is a plus for an owner-seller, who can meet and greet strangers, listen to their comments, and respond to negative comments about the house with positives. It helps to have a knowledge of financing as well as connections with lenders if you're acting as your own agent, especially if your property is marketed to first-time home buyers. They need someone to hold their hands through all the phases of qualifying for a loan and then processing the application and forms. That sales expertise also comes into play when the deal is finalized and loose ends need tying and contracts need signing. If you think about selling by owner, definitely plan to hire a real estate lawyer to represent you so you leave nothing to chance.

Tax Advantage After the Sale

One of the big advantages of owning real estate is how favorably it is treated by the tax code. We have been able to use this to our advantage over the 30 years or so that we have been working on houses. During this time the tax laws have changed, and no doubt they are going to change in the future, but the favorable treatment of home ownership has survived.

Owner Occupied

If you live in a house you own and sell it, the first $250,000 for an individual or $500,000 for a couple is tax-free. The current law allows you to do this every two years. Just how long you have to live in the house is open to some question, but usually when we lived in a house it took a few years to completely renovate it and get it back on the market. Our strategy is to live in a house that has the greatest potential for profit.

Nonowner Occupied

If you don't live in the property but hold it for more than a year while you are working on it, the gain on the sale can qualify as a capital gain. Capital gains are taxed at a 20 percent rate, which may be lower than your current tax rate. In either case, the profit from the sale will not be taxed at a higher rate than your overall tax bracket rate. This will hold up unless you buy and sell so many properties that the IRS considers you a dealer, and then you must pay straight tax.

Rental Property

Rental property can be traded for like property, and no tax on the transaction will be due. This has tax advantages, but so far we haven't used the strategy. There are plenty of books on the subject and tax advisers out there with this information.

Tax Savings Are Not Enough

The most important point about taxes is to remember that property must sell for a profit for you to save on taxes. Buying property and selling it for a loss may be a great tax write-off, but it makes for a poor business plan. The real estate investments you make must stand on their own merits. If there is not a positive cash flow resulting from the deal, then it's not worth doing. The tax breaks that are available increase the amount of the profit you get to keep, but tax breaks alone don't generate profits.

CHAPTER 16

TIMELINE FOR A FAST FIX IT AND FLIP (UNDER 60 DAYS)

This timeline is for making various cosmetic improvements to a three-bedroom ranch located in a good neighborhood. It had been rental property and showed signs of neglect by both the renters and landlord. While the house was standard issue, we saw its potential because of its location and attractive stone fireplace in the living room. The house was on a quarter-acre lot with dense, overgrown bushes and shrubbery and a foot-high lawn. The exterior siding and windows were vinyl-clad and in good condition, but a deck off the back of the house had been covered with outdoor carpeting that rotted the decking.

Inside, the rooms were all painted yellow. The living room, hall, and three bedrooms were all carpeted in a worn, rust-colored carpeting, and there was a patch of chipped and broken ceramic tile at the entry. The carpeting held the smells of pets who had previously occupied the house, making it a real turnoff to potential buyers. The kitchen and dining area had a wild-patterned green and yellow vinyl floor. The wooden cabinets and laminate countertop were in acceptable condition. The bathroom had wall tile with a bathtub and toilet in acceptable condition. At least half of the electrical switches and receptacles had to be replaced because they were caked with layers of paint, and those in the kitchen and bathroom would not meet the building codes.

Measure-and-Make-Notes Visit

Before closing on the property and taking possession, we had an afternoon to assess the property. During this measure-and-make-notes visit, we took room measurements and determined the specific improvements and upgrades to make.

After the visit we made initial calls to price and order a Dumpster. We had delivery scheduled for our first week in the house so we could fill it with all the things we tore out. This included the carpeting, padding, flooring, and other materials; debris left in the yard; and piles of tree and shrubbery branches that we had left over after pruning and grooming.

In the weeks before taking possession we made several shopping trips to home centers, flooring outlets, and hardware stores to explore styles, colors, and prices of carpeting, vinyl flooring, lighting fixtures, kitchen appliances, and replacements for the bathroom.

We both planned to work on the house full-time along with hiring two specialty contractors: one to rebuild the deck and another to make repairs from termite damage to the south wall of the house. Before closing on the property we made initial calls to contractors to get estimates and schedule the work for when we were there working on the house. We had both contractors come with us on the walk-through, and we discussed what had to be done to repair the wall and deck. The carpenter repairing the sill and foundation decided that all the work could be done from the outside of the house. Only the lower portion of the wall was affected, so the siding could be removed and the damaged portion of the wall studs and sill repaired and the siding replaced. The deck builder was also going to work outside the house, so our work inside the house wouldn't be affected by either of them.

We ordered cleaning supplies and off-white latex paint in five-gallon containers for walls and ceiling (flat) and trim (semigloss). We organized the tools and equipment we thought we would need so it would be ready as soon as we took possession. This included a garbage can, plastic garbage bags, hand tool box, ladder, shop vacuum, demolition tools, garden hose, lawn mower and pruning tools, work light, power tools, heavy-duty extension cords, and work horses. We planned to set up two staging areas: one with a source of water for paint cleanup and another area to store tools and materials.

Week 1

The goal for the first week was to fill the Dumpster and get rid of unwanted materials and appliances. The longer we kept the Dumpster the more it cost, so we planned to fill it as quickly as possible with the yard waste after extensive pruning and cutting back of the overgrown landscape. Then we loaded it with trash and debris that was left on the property. The projects inside and out didn't affect each other, and depending on the weather, we could revise our work plan.

Day 1

- Checked all doors and windows for operation or repair work and noted on checklist
- Changed the exterior door locks
- Removed bathroom vanity and faucet, medicine cabinet, light fixture, and floor and ceiling registers
- Disconnected and moved refrigerator and range to the Dumpster
- Took down and threw out all draperies, shades, and hardware; shower curtain and rod
- Removed all base shoe molding around the rooms for a better-fitting new-carpet installation; tossed molding (not worth saving) in the Dumpster
- Tore up and removed all wall-to-wall carpeting and padding in living room, hall, and three bedrooms, including the old carpeting tracks and some tacks left in the floor from previous installations
- Chipped out and removed a three-by-five-foot ceramic tile pad in living room at entry

Day 2

- Removed vinyl flooring and adhesive in kitchen and laundry
- Vacuumed all windows and floors
- Mowed "first-cut" lawn and raked up clippings
- Made second pass with mower and raked up clippings
- Began pruning row of shrubbery lining the sides of the property

Day 3

- Continued pruning shrubbery lining the sides of the property
- Removed debris left in backyard and shed (rotten landscape timbers, broken lawn furniture, car tires, old grill, and rusty yard tools and mower)
- Pruned four trees
- Checked all electrical switches and receptacles to see if they worked or needed to be replaced; removed all switch plate covers and marked their location on the back side; made count for new plate covers and replacement devices needed

Day 4

- Pruned all evergreens in front of house
- Pruned all shrubbery across the rear of the property
- Looked for bare spots in lawn and weeded, seeded, and watered
- Edged all garden beds

Day 5

- Throughout the house removed window hardware and interior door lock sets, washed all surfaces, and let dry
- Throughout the house removed all ceiling light fixtures
- Installed new switches and outlets where needed, then covered all switches and receptacles with masking tape to protect from paint

Week 2

This week's goal was to get the interior of the house ready to paint. Patching and priming the interior was a major job because many of the walls required at least two applications of wallboard compound. The same was true for woodwork and trim. Because the walls and wood-work were painted yellow, everything needed a prime coat before painting. Removing the black mastic that held some cork tiles to the dining room wall presented the biggest challenge.

Day 6

- Laid down drop cloths on all floors
- Applied wide masking tape along fireplace walls to protect from paint
- Prepared walls and ceiling in living room, hall, and three bedrooms by removing nails and filling holes, cracks, and nail pops with first application of wallboard compound and let dry
- Prepared woodwork and trim around windows and doors in living room, hall, and three bedrooms by filling in holes and cracks with interior spackling compound and let dry

Day 7

- In living room, hall, and three bedrooms, sanded first applications of compounds filling the wallboard and woodwork, then made second application to fill in voids and let dry
- In kitchen-dining area laid down drop cloths on countertop
- Removed cork tiles on dining area wall and used heat gun on black mastic adhesive
- Made repairs to holes and structural crack uncovered in cork wall
- Applied stain killer to black spots left by mastic adhesive on cork wall

Day 8

- Sanded repairs to cork wall and applied skim coat of drywall compound
- In living room, hall, and three bedrooms, sanded second applications of compounds filling the wallboard and woodwork
- Prepared walls and ceiling in kitchen-dining area by removing nails and filling holes, cracks, and nail pops with first application of wallboard compound and let dry

- Prepared woodwork and trim around windows and doors in kitchen-dining area by filling in holes and cracks with interior spackling compound and let dry
- Applied wide masking tape around cabinets to protect from primer and paint

Day 9

- Sanded skim coat of drywall compound on cork wall and made second application of compound
- In kitchen-dining area sanded first applications of compounds in walls, ceilings, and woodwork, then made second application to fill in voids and let dry
- Removed all switch and receptacle covers in kitchen and replaced outlets with GFCIs and new switches
- Wrapped masking tape around outlets and switches to protect from paint

Day 10

- Sanded cork wall skim coat and all walls, ceilings, and woodwork in kitchen-dining area
- Vacuumed all walls, ceilings, woodwork, and floors
- Washed exterior of kitchen cabinets
- Shook out drop cloths and put back in place
- Applied latex PVA primer to walls and ceilings in living room, hall, three bedrooms, and kitchen-dining area

Week 3

The goals for this week were getting a final coat of paint on all the rooms and woodwork around doors and windows, including the closet and room doors, and beginning work in the bathroom.

Day 11

- Applied first coat of paint to ceilings and walls in living room, hall, three bedrooms

Day 12

- Applied final coat of paint to ceilings and walls in the kitchen-dining area
- Applied first coat of paint to woodwork and trim in living room, hall, three bedrooms

Day 13

- Applied second coat of paint to woodwork and trim in living room, hall, three bedrooms

Day 14

- Applied first coat of paint to woodwork and trim in kitchen-dining area
- Prepared bathroom by washing the ceiling, painted and tiled walls, window trim, and door
- Made first application of epoxy repair system to rebuild the rotten windowsill in tub surround

Day 15

- Applied second coat of paint to woodwork and trim in kitchen-dining area
- Scrubbed the bathtub, tiles, grout, and faucet
- Removed indoor carpeting tiles on bathroom floor
- Sanded epoxy and made second application to windowsill

Week 4

This week's goals were to complete the bathroom and make repairs to the exterior doors.

Day 16

- Applied masking tape on edge of bathroom wall tiles to protect them from paint
- Sanded the second application of epoxy to windowsill and applied primer
- Repaired exterior trim around patio door by scraping wood trim, priming bare spots, filling in holes and sanding; also cleaned out track so panels would slide freely
- Replaced handle on interior of patio door
- Removed door knob and knocker of front door
- Vacuumed and cleaned entryway threshold

Day 17

- Painted walls, ceiling in bathroom
- Sanded wood trim around patio door and painted
- Used heat gun to remove layers of paint on front door

Day 18

- Painted window trim and door in bathroom
- Filled in holes and cracks in front door
- Washed walls and trim and filled in holes in laundry area

Day 19

- Installed new vanity and faucet, shower curtain rod, medicine cabinet, and light fixture in bathroom; replaced toilet seat
- Installed new ceiling and floor registers throughout the house
- Washed bathroom floor

- Repaired tracks on bedroom closet doors
- Installed smoke and CO detectors
- Mowed lawn

Day 20

- Sanded surface of front door and applied primer
- Washed interior of kitchen cabinets and lined with shelf paper
- Cleaned dishwasher
- Vacuumed furnace and replaced filter
- Washed utility area around hot-water heater

Week 5

At the beginning of the week the goal was to finish up most of our work in preparation for the carpeting and flooring installation. Then the objectives were to complete cleaning the exterior and make final installations of light fixtures and window blinds and to install the kitchen floor before the refrigerator and range were delivered.

Day 21

- Painted ceiling, walls, and trim in laundry room
- Painted front door
- Installed new lighting fixtures throughout the house
- Installed new house number plaque on siding

Day 22

- Washed laundry room floor
- Cleaned out gutters and installed new splash blocks
- Power washed siding
- Repaired torn screens
- Had carpeting installed in the living room, hall, and three bedrooms
- Installed new knocker on front door

Day 23

- Had vinyl flooring installed in kitchen and dining areas
- Trimmed doors that were too tight on the new carpeting
- Installed new hardware on interior doors
- Washed all windows inside and out
- Painted base shoe molding for kitchen and dining room floors
- Installed new window miniblinds

Day 24

- Installed new base shoe molding in kitchen and dining area and touched up paint as needed
- Hooked up new range and refrigerator
- Installed new vertical blind on patio glider door
- Mowed lawn
- Removed all painting equipment

Day 25

- Removed all tools and materials
- Invited real estate listing broker to view house

TIMELINE FOR A SPACE-EXPANDING MAKEOVER THAT INCREASED RESALE VALUE (SIX MONTHS)

This timeline features an expandable two-bedroom Cape Cod with an unfinished attic. The work involved improving and redecorating the first floor of the house, which included a living room, dining room, kitchen, bath, utility room, and two bedrooms. Then we built a dormer, creating two bedrooms, a hall, and a bathroom upstairs. The exterior of the house was given a coat of paint, making it appear totally new from the outside. We transformed the house from a two bedroom, one-bath home to one with four bedrooms and two baths. The work took approximately five months to complete, and it was put on the market in the sixth month.

The house was unusual in that it had been owned by a woman who was a hoarder. Every room was filled waist-high with furniture and piles of stuff. It was difficult to see the walls of the house, let alone the floors, because the rooms were overstuffed with furniture that was stacked with piles of newspapers, magazines, old clothing, and just about anything else under the sun.

Before taking possession, we ordered a Dumpster to be delivered and hired two helpers to sort through all the stuff that had been left there. We invited everyone we knew to come and take what they wanted. Goodwill picked up some of the furnishings, and some things were donated to charity, but most of the objects were destined to fill three Dumpsters.

We removed the refrigerator (filled with spoiled food), range, and flooring in the kitchen, and the vanity, medicine cabinet, and flooring in the bathroom. Throughout the house we removed draperies, window shades, and carpeting.

The exterior of the house was also laden with debris and miscellaneous car engines and parts. The lawn and shrubbery were overgrown, but there was salvageable low shrubbery that framed the front door and side entrance. The driveway was a patchwork of asphalt that needed repairs and resurfacing.

It took two weeks to completely empty the house and tame the yard. We were surprised to find that the walls and floors were actually in pretty fair shape. There was mildew in areas of the bathroom and kitchen, but the walls were sound and the oak floors were worn but could be restored by refinishing.

Because the attic was also filled to capacity, we had to wait until the second week to measure the space and assess the additional space we planned to build. We knew the house had been built for expansion because the heating ducts were installed but capped off. The stairs were wide and in the center of the house, so the layout of the second floor was easy to determine. At the top of the stairs we designed a hall with the new bathroom over the first-floor bathroom and a bedroom on either side of it.

We painted the living room, dining room, and hall in a flat, off-white latex paint and used a satin finish on the woodwork and trim. We hung wallpaper in the two bedrooms downstairs and the kitchen and painted all the new rooms upstairs in the same off-white.

We did most of the work ourselves, occasionally hiring helpers when needed. We hired a roofing contractor to reroof the entire house and had a flooring retailer install the carpeting.

Month 1

The top priority was to remove the clutter and debris inside and around the property. Then the objective was to plan and design the layout of the attic expansion and apply for a building permit. While waiting for the permit, the goal was to work on cleaning and decorating the first floor. Here is a rough timeline of how the work progressed.

Weeks 1 and 2

- Checked all doors and windows to see if they were operational; opened windows to air out house; changed the exterior door locks
- Removed contents from the house and yard, filling three Dumpsters
- Took measurements of the attic

Week 3

- Designed a floor plan for the dormer and attic expansion
- Made an application for a building permit to expand second floor
- Measured rooms to estimate and order painting and wallpaper supplies
- Set up two staging areas: a wet workstation in the utility room with washtub for cleaning out paint brushes and rollers and storing paint, and a dry workstation in the living room to store tools, materials, and radio
- Brought in cleaning supplies, power tools, work horses, garbage bags, hand tool box, ladder, shop vacuum, demolition tools, garden hose, lawn mower, and pruning gear
- Vacuumed all windows and floors
- Throughout the house checked all electrical switches and receptacles to see if they worked or needed to be replaced; made a count of new plate covers and replacement devices needed
- Laid down drop cloths in all rooms on first floor
- Throughout the house removed window hardware, doorknobs, and lock sets and cleaned and polished them
- Throughout the house removed all ceiling light fixtures and replaced with temporary light fixtures
- Mowed the lawn

Week 4

- Removed wallpaper in two bedrooms and dining room
- Washed walls in two bedrooms and dining room to remove adhesive and washed windows, doors, woodwork, and trim
- Prepped ceiling in two bedrooms by filling cracks and nail pops with first application of wallboard compound and let dry
- Prepped windows, doors, woodwork, and baseboard trim in two bedrooms by filling in holes and cracks with interior spackling compound and let dry
- Sanded first applications of compounds filling the ceiling, woodwork, and trim; then made second application to fill in voids and let dry
- Sanded second application of compounds on bedroom ceilings, windows, doors, woodwork, and trim
- Painted ceilings in two bedrooms
- Painted doors, windows, woodwork, and trim in two bedrooms
- Applied sizing to two bedroom walls
- Hung wallpaper in two bedrooms
- Worked out final details of second-floor addition with the Building Department
- Mowed the lawn

Month 2

The goal was to clean and decorate most of the rooms on the first floor. Although it was a small eat-in kitchen, it required considerable time because we painted the cabinets, which needed extensive preparation and sanding. We also made out the materials list for the second-floor addition.

Week 5

- Prepped walls and ceilings in living room, dining room, and hall by removing nails and filling holes, cracks, and nail pops with first application of wallboard compound and let dry

- Prepped doors, windows, woodwork, and trim in living room, dining room, and hall by filling in holes and cracks with interior spackling compound and let dry
- Sanded first application of wallboard compound in living room, dining room, and hall and made second application to fill voids and let dry
- Sanded first applications of spackling compound in living room, dining room, and hall windows, woodwork, and trim and made second application to fill in voids and let dry
- Sanded second applications of compounds on the ceilings, walls, woodwork, and trim in living room, dining room, and hall
- Removed all switch plate covers and marked their location on the back side
- Installed replacement switches and GFCI receptacles and wrapped with masking tape to protect from paint
- Painted ceilings and walls in living room, dining room, and hall
- Mowed the lawn and trimmed shrubbery

Week 6

- Painted doors, windows, woodwork, and trim in living room, dining room, and hall
- Reinstalled door and window hardware in living room, dining room, hall, and bedrooms
- Removed all switch and receptacle covers in kitchen and replaced outlets with GFCIs and new switches
- Removed wallpaper in kitchen
- Washed kitchen ceiling, walls, windows, doors, woodwork, and trim
- Washed kitchen cabinets inside and out
- Repaired ceiling in kitchen by removing nails and filling holes, cracks, and nail pops with first application of wallboard compound and let dry
- Applied wallboard compound to large cracks in kitchen wall discovered when wallpaper was removed and let dry
- Sanded first application of wallboard compound on kitchen ceiling and applied second coat and let dry

- Sanded first application of wallboard compound to cracks in kitchen wall and applied second coat of wallboard compound to cracks in kitchen wall with coat of PVA primer
- Sanded second coat of wallboard compound on ceiling
- Painted the kitchen ceiling

Week 7

- Prepped cabinets, windows, doors, woodwork, and trim in kitchen by filling in holes and cracks with interior spackling compound and let dry
- Sanded first application of spackling compound on cabinets, windows, doors, woodwork, and trim and made second application
- Sanded second coat of spackling compound on cabinets, windows, doors, woodwork, and trim
- Applied wallpaper sizing to kitchen walls
- Finished sanding the exterior of the kitchen cabinets
- Primed the kitchen cabinets inside and out
- Primed the kitchen windows, doors, woodwork, and trim
- Painted the kitchen cabinets inside and out
- Painted the kitchen windows, doors, woodwork, and trim
- Mowed the lawn

Week 8

- Repaired the garbage disposal
- Hung wallpaper in the kitchen
- Installed new cabinet hardware
- Installed new countertop
- Installed new kitchen light fixture
- Installed new range with vent hood
- Installed new refrigerator
- Removed wallpaper in bathroom
- Washed ceiling, walls, window, door, and trim in bathroom

Month 3

The goal was to complete the bathroom and refinish the floors on the first floor and then make preparations to begin working on the rough framing on the second floor.

Week 9

- Checked the second-floor drawings
- Ordered lumber and materials for attic
- Painted bathroom ceiling
- Painted bathroom walls, window, door, and trim
- Installed new floor tiles in bathroom
- Installed new vanity and faucet in bathroom
- Replaced receptacles with GFCI devices in bathroom and utility room
- Installed new toilet in bathroom
- Installed new light fixture and wall accessories in bathroom
- Washed ceiling, walls, window, and door in utility room
- Painted ceiling, walls, window, and door in utility room
- Replaced washtub in utility room
- Mowed the lawn

Week 10

- First rough-sanded, then fine-sanded, and then applied a penetrating sealer to hardwood floors in living room, dining room, hall, and two bedrooms
- Installed new floor tiles in kitchen and utility room
- Displayed building permit in window
- Protected refinished floor in hall leading to attic stairs with drop cloths
- Assembled carpentry tools and equipment on the second floor

Week 11

- Built rough framing for the dormer front wall with windows
- Cut into roof and removed sheathing, shingles, and rafters
- Moved front wall into position
- Installed new roof rafters and plywood sheathing on rafters, and enclosed sides of dormer
- Put exterior fascia and trim on dormers
- Mowed the lawn

Week 12

- Roofers patched dormer into existing roof, then reroofed entire house
- Built rough framing for two bedrooms, hall, and bathroom
- Opened heating ducts in knee wall
- Installed subfloor to second floor
- Insulated second-floor walls and ceilings
- Roughed in new plumbing lines for second floor bathroom and installed bathtub

Month 4

The goal was to complete the work in the new second-floor rooms by running the electrical wiring and installing and painting the wallboard.

Week 13

- Ran electrical lines to the second floor for hall and bedroom lighting, switches, and receptacles and bathroom lighting/fan, GFCI receptacles, and switches
- Passed inspection of plumbing and electrical rough-in work before installing wallboard
- Installed wallboard panels in all rooms on second floor
- Mowed the lawn

Week 14

- Applied the wallboard tape and mud to wallboard panels in all rooms on second floor
- Sanded all wallboard joint seams, reapplied compound, and sanded
- Installed doors and window trim and baseboard in all second-floor rooms
- Primed and painted ceilings and walls in two bedrooms, hall, and bathroom

Week 15

- Primed and painted windows, doors, woodwork, and trim
- Installed doors and lock sets in second-floor rooms
- Installed ceiling light fixtures in hall, two bedrooms, and bathroom
- Installed vinyl tiles in new second-floor bathroom
- Installed tile in bathtub surround
- Mowed the lawn

Week 16

- Installed toilet, vanity and faucet, medicine cabinet, light-vent, and accessories
- Had installers lay carpeting on stairs, second-floor hall, and second-floor bedrooms
- Installed miniblinds in living room, dining room, bathrooms, and bedrooms
- Installed handrail in staircase
- Had final inspection completed by building inspector

Month 5

The last month of the project involved a face-lift for the exterior of the house by painting and adding shutters and working on the driveway and final cleanup projects.

Week 17

- Removed storm windows and cleaned all windowsills and sashes on the exterior
- Scraped and sanded exterior of windows and trim
- Scraped and sanded siding
- Primed new siding on dormer
- Spot primed windows and trim
- Mowed the lawn

Week 18

- Painted all siding and the dormer
- Painted all windows and trim

Week 19

- Installed vinyl window shutters
- Cleaned and refastened loose gutters
- Scraped and sanded front and back doors
- Primed front and back doors
- Painted front and back doors
- Mowed the lawn

Week 20

- Installed a new front storm door
- Added new house numbers and mailbox
- Washed windows throughout house
- Edged garden beds

- Patched driveway and applied driveway sealer
- Mowed the lawn
- Invited real estate broker to tour house

Month 6

- Placed house on the market
- Mowed the lawn

CHAPTER 18

TIMELINE FOR A LIVE-IN, FIX-UP, AND SELL-LATER HOUSE (365-PLUS DAYS)

This timeline outlines improvements we made to a historic house. It was a folk Victorian built in the late 1800s and filled with charm and architectural appeal, but it was neglected and inappropriately modernized by previous owners. The location of the house was ideal—a tree-lined street complete with old-fashioned streetlights and other historic homes. Most of the houses in the neighborhood had been restored from the ground up, meaning the costly foundation work and replacement of sills was done. Our house was one of the smallest on the block, surely the poor cousin of the lovely restored homes in the neighborhood that sported updated kitchens and baths and nicely painted facades.

The house had been rental property with an out-of-town owner, so the interior needed considerable work. A previous owner had invested in a new foundation and repaired the house's sills. The interior work involved all of the rooms, so the plan was all-encompassing to bring the house back to its original charm and character.

The House

The house had a living room, dining room, large kitchen, and utility room on the first floor and three bedrooms and a bathroom upstairs. The small size and strange configuration of the bedroom adjacent to the bathroom made it more of a closet than a bedroom. The bathroom, while serviceable, occupied much too much space. The house originally did not have central heat or plumbing, and both of these conveniences were probably added in the early 1950s. Most of the pipes supplying the hot-water baseboard heat were visible. Outside the house was a wide porch across the front and a nice side porch off the kitchen. The house was sided in aluminum siding with its original shutters.

The appeal of the house was its architectural elements: a handsome staircase with intricate banister and spindles and fish scale detail on the sides of the staircase, a wood-burning fireplace in the dining room, and a wood stove in the living room. Throughout the house there were floor-to-ceiling windows with one-of-a-kind molded casings and heavy four-panel doors.

On the minus side, the second floor had crater-size cracks in the plaster walls and ceilings and painted pine floorboards in all the rooms and staircase. Previous owners had "modernized" the living room with two hopper windows, and a 1950s-style pass-through in the dining room cut into the kitchen. The improvements required extensive restoration and work throughout the house and modernization in the kitchen and bathrooms.

The Challenge

We had to carve out space for living, working, eating, and sleeping while making the improvements. Living in a construction zone requires considerable patience and stamina and certainly not an ounce of pride, because you have to ignore what visitors think when they see your living conditions. A shop vacuum on both floors is necessary for the ongoing exercise of removing dust and dirt from exposed wall studs, beams, and flooring.

Camping under duress is the closest analogy that comes to mind. You are not enjoying the great outdoors, but you are under considerable stress and uncertainty. It's not for everyone. Living in a work in progress also requires a continual outlay of energy and funds, so a long-term plan is important to give yourself a clear idea of the results when it will be over.

The Plan

During the first three months of possession we worked full-time on the house; after that we worked on it piecemeal, scheduled around our writing business and other investment properties that we owned and managed.

Year 1

We hired a pest-control company to flea-bomb the house and eradicate the flea population before we could move in; then we put most of our furnishings and possessions into storage. We moved into the house with only the bare minimum of furniture needed to live, eat, and work in the house. We set up a small but working household on the first floor.

Phase 1: Demolish Second-Floor Rooms, Landing, and Hall

The first phase included the heavy and dirty work of tearing out the plaster walls on the second floor. First we removed all the doors, window trim, and woodwork and marked them on the back so we could reinstall them later. Then we broke up and removed all the old plaster walls and plastic plywood that covered some of them. We hired a helper with a truck to haul away the debris.

We cleaned up all debris and plaster dust and set up bedroom furniture in the open space. We drove nails onto exposed wall studs for clothes hooks—very handy, indeed.

Phase 2: Attack First Floor

In the dining room we removed the wooden ledge and pass-through that opened into the kitchen and filled the hole with wallboard. We taped all joints and then applied wallboard compound and let it dry; we repeated the process until the patched area was smooth and flush with the surface of the wall. We primed and painted the ceiling, wainscoting, doors, windows, woodwork, and trim and hung wallpaper above the wainscoting.

In the kitchen we removed layers of old wallpaper and primed and painted the ceiling, doors, windows, woodwork, and trim. We applied sizing to the walls and then hung wallpaper. We scrubbed the kitchen cabinets inside and out and applied an oil finish to rejuvenate them. We removed layers of old flooring and hired an installer to lay a new sub-floor and vinyl sheet flooring.

In the living room we removed the hopper windows in the end wall and primed and painted the ceiling, doors, windows, woodwork, and trim. We removed the old wood stove, which was cracked, and built a new tile hearth for a new one we had installed. We hired a floor sander to refinish the original pine floors in the living room, hall, and dining room and set up a minimum of furniture in the living room.

Phase 3: Attack Second Floor

We redesigned the bedrooms to accommodate larger closets (originals were not deep enough for hangers). We hired an electrician to rewire the second floor with new switches, receptacles, closet and overhead lighting, and three-way switch controls for the staircase. We installed insulation in all the exterior walls.

In an effort to create a smaller-footprint bathroom, we eliminated the claw-footed tub and shower stall in exchange for a tub/shower. We gave the tub to a friend and still have memories of sliding the heavy brute down the staircase and watching it come close to breaking through the front door. We enlarged the adjoining bedroom with space from the bathroom.

In the bathroom we installed a tub/shower unit with a tile surround and light, toilet, vanity, and light/vent unit in the ceiling. We cut down the Corian countertop from the old bathroom to reuse it and installed a mirror over the vanity. We also installed new flooring and wallpaper.

Year 2

This year the push was to make the second floor of the house a bit more livable, which meant hanging drywall, repairing the windows, rein-stalling the baseboard heating to conceal the piping, and adding stor-age space.

The Second Floor

We stripped multiple layers of paint from all the second-floor window woodwork, trim, and doors and then sanded all of it. We scraped and sanded all window sashes and rebuilt the window frames. We framed out all the room and closet doorjambs.

We removed all exposed hot-water heating pipes and reinstalled them to be concealed by new wallboard. In each bedroom we installed zone valves and thermostats. We added foldaway stairs to the attic to increase storage area and reinforced the attic floor with sheathing tied into the rafters. In the attic we increased the amount of loose-fill insulation.

We hired a drywall contractor to hang, tape, and sand wallboard in all the rooms on the second floor and the hall and stairway. We primed and painted all the new wallboard.

The First Floor

We hired a finish carpenter to design and build a bookcase with cabinets on both sides of the wood stove. We installed new storm/screen doors at the front and rear of the house and built a custom-size screen for the porch door.

Year 3

We finished the detail work to complete the living space on the second floor, finished decorating in the living room, and had a small addition built to replace the utility room.

Second Floor

We reinstalled the window trim and woodwork on the second floor and primed and painted it. We did the same with the old doors. We painted staircase spindles, stair risers, and fish scale molding and refinished the natural handrail.

We hired a floor sander to sand and refinish the painted pine floorboards in the hall, landing, and stairs. We hired a carpeting installer to lay wall-to-wall carpeting in the three bedrooms.

First Floor

We primed and painted the bookcase-cabinet in the living room. We rebuilt and painted the deck off the back porch because it was damaged and rotting in places.

The utility room off the kitchen was rotting away and sinking into the ground, and the furnace was on its last leg. We designed an addition to replace the utility room with a laundry-utility room and a three-quarter bathroom. The addition included a new furnace with storage closet and a laundry area with a closet. We hired a contractor to build the addition, install the furnace, build the walls, and rough in the bathroom plumbing. We painted the ceiling, walls, and trim in the addition and installed the new bathroom fixtures and wall accessories.

With all its improvements, the house has taken on a new personality, and today it stands proud and polished in its neighborhood of traditional homes. Inflation as well as the improvements we made have increased its value, to be sure.

Living in a house that's under renovation is an experience that's not for everyone, but it's truly amazing how quickly one forgets just how bad the conditions were. Ask anyone who has rehabbed a house while living there, and they often laugh at the fact that they've forgotten the anguish and unpleasant conditions. They're glad it's over and most do not want to repeat the process. But there will always be some who admire old houses, and who relish the challenge of finding a neglected old house and restoring it to its original splendor.

INDEX